Father Madden's

LIFE OF CHRIST

Father Madden's

LIFE OF CHRIST

by RICHARD R. MADDEN, o.c.d.
AUTHOR OF *Men in Sandals*

THE BRUCE PUBLISHING COMPANY
MILWAUKEE

NIHIL OBSTAT QUOMINUS IMPRIMATUR 17 JUNII 1959:

FR. MICHAEL A S. FAMILIA, O.C.D.
FR. DIONYSIUS A S. FAMILIA, O.C.D.

IMPRIMI POTEST:

FR. ALBERTUS A SS. SACRAMENTO, O.C.D.
Provincialis

NIHIL OBSTAT:

JOHN F. MURPHY, S.T.D.
Censor librorum

IMPRIMATUR:

✠ WILLIAM E. COUSINS
Archbishop of Milwaukee

January 20, 1960

Library of Congress Catalog Card Number: 60–10205

MADE IN THE UNITED STATES OF AMERICA

DEDICATION

To the youth of America
who have lent so much warmth
and enchantment to my life

ACKNOWLEDGMENTS

A couple of years ago a valiant little woman, Henriette Mackin by name, pressured me ever so lightly to do a Life of Christ for *Hi Time Magazine*. I am grateful that she did. I have enriched my own life by writing it; I hope that my teen-age friends will enrich theirs by reading it. But good or bad, Miss Mackin and *Hi Time Magazine* are responsible.

When it came time to type up the manuscript, the only two people I could find were two very busy little housewives, Corky Lynch and Rita Ryan. What with all the other pressing duties of a very trying and complicated vocation, namely, raising children and keeping their husbands fat and happy, they still came up with the finished product. They are like other Marys in giving this particular Christ to youth. May He never forget their contribution. They are responsible for this book.

Finally, in my retreat work for teen-agers throughout the country, I have been continually badgered by them to "tell us more about Christ." Therefore, they too are responsible.

Just about the only person who is not responsible for this book is the author.

CONTENTS

Father Madden's

LIFE OF CHRIST

1 THE ONE-MAN REVOLUTION

The Sea of Galilee lay placid under the rays of the morning sun, sparkling like a giant blue diamond fourteen miles long and seven wide. The Man stepped from the shadows and walked across the beach to the water's edge. With magnificent, quiet eyes, He watched a big fisherman busily working with his nets. After a few moments He came to a decision about what He was to do, and there was a slight, playful smile upon His lips. He raised His hand in greeting as the fisherman looked up.

What Simon saw took his breath away. It was not the tall gauntness of the Man. It wasn't the tangle of His beard or the hard brownness of His skin. It must have been those eyes. And the words He spoke. The simple stark words that triggered the beginning of the great new revolution. "Follow Me."

Right then, so far as Simon the fisherman was concerned, there was nothing else in the world – no fish, no nets, no boat, no lake. Only the strange eyes of the strange Man. And the words. The invitation. So there was nothing else that Simon could do. There was nothing else in his life then but this Man, just down from the hills of Capharnaum.

Without counting the cost, without caring who would mend his nets or tend his boat, without worrying about the needs of his wife or mother-in-law, Simon let himself be enslaved by the eyes and the voice of the Son of God. Dropping his fishing gear into the bottom of the boat and rubbing his hard hands together to dry them, he hurried with his brother Andrew to the side of Christ.

A short walk along the shore brought them to James and John. These two fell in step. They were a group of ordinary men, hardly distinguishable from any other – but they were a new breed on a new mission. No longer men seeking after fish, but fishermen seeking after men!

Who was this Man who drew the fishermen into His ranks? He was not a complete stranger because Peter, James, and John had seen Him before. They had spoken with Him. That was the day on which they stood listening to the street preacher, John the Baptist, speaking of the one "who was to come, the Lord whom you know not, the latchet of whose shoe I am not worthy to loose." At that moment, the years of the hidden life fell away and Christ made His first public appearance before the world. John the Baptist saw Him coming down the street; he pointed to Him and said, "Behold the Lamb of God."

Later, Andrew told Peter, James, and John. They visited with Christ. They listened to Him speak. They walked with

Him. But it was only a temporary thing. The Master was pumping them, screening them, drawing them out.

Now, two months later, He was ready. So He went after them. When He said, "Follow Me," on the shores of the lake that day, He was not fooling. This was for keeps; it was forever. And they knew it. They went with Him happily. They turned their backs on the life that was theirs, to live instead the life that was His.

The Apostles were thrilled at their newly discovered Friend, but they did not really know who He was. They should have known Him, but they didn't. They should have been expecting Him because He did not come unannounced. More than four hundred distinct prophecies had foretold His arrival. History tells of many men who appeared on the stage of life, claiming, "I am from God" – but nobody else told us they were coming. Yet, through a period of 2000 years before His coming, we were told by the prophets where He would appear and how, under what circumstances He would be born, what He would do, and how He would die. And the prophets were never wrong. The facts of the New Testament are but the fulfillment of what is written by the prophets in the Old Testament.

Down through the centuries, the prophets were men enlightened by God to foretell events. They were the interpreters, the spokesmen of God, making known God's will to the Jewish people. They were not quacks, soothsayers, or fortunetellers. Their mission was divine. They were always right because God would never have permitted them to spread, in His name, any falsehoods or erroneous interpretations.

Seven hundred years before the birth of Christ, the prophet Isaias (7:14) said, "Behold a virgin shall conceive and bear a son and His name shall be called Emmanuel."

Isaias was right about that. Micheas foretold His being born in Bethlehem. And David wrote of Him, "They have pierced My hands and My feet; they have numbered all My bones. They divide My garments among them and for My vesture, they cast lots." And David was exactly right.

Yes, the world should have recognized Him when He came, but it didn't. Which proves how stupid we can be. He was born in a little isolated village just outside of Jerusalem. He grew up in Nazareth, another tiny village about sixty miles to the north. He never wrote a book. Never went to college. Never held any public office. He never, in fact, traveled more than two hundred miles from the place where He was born. So nobody knew Him.

But they would. He was the Messias, the Promised One who came into the world to destroy its sins, who, by His death, would reopen the gates of heaven. They didn't know Him then, but they would. Men would throw away their calendars and begin measuring the days as if time began the moment He was born. He would remake mankind. He would tear down the old laws of hatred and install the new laws of love. He would give a rebirth to the poor, the weak, the sinful. He would, in general, "renew the face of the earth."

We know what Christ wanted to do. Man, in the persons of Adam and Eve, had offended an infinite God. Only an infinite God could make proper atonement for such crime. Such was the work of Jesus. So He had come to earth to lift the world up from the squalor of its ignorance and its sin. He had come to redeem, and to save, and to teach. This we know.

The extraordinary thing about it is the method that He chose to use. He would not monopolize the work. He would not do it all Himself. He would share it with His creatures.

He would call upon the men and women of every age to join Him. He would say to all of us, "Help Me do My work. Help Me bring salvation to all the world."

These fishermen were His first students in His first school. If they were to do His work, they had to learn. He was their object lesson. He wanted them to see with His eyes (more than with their own) all the sheep without a shepherd, the fields white with harvest, and not merely an annoying mob of undisciplined and ignorant people. He wanted them to feel with His heart. He wanted His hands to be theirs. He wanted His cravings, His longings, His prayers to be their own, so that when they acted they would act in Him and for Him.

Indeed, He went about His Father's business, but He didn't go it alone. He called upon Peter and the others, and He does the same today. He uses us. He needs us – in order that the world might know Him. He has given us a lamp to carry through the darkness of earth. The lamp is ours. He gave it to us. But the light of the lamp belongs to the world – and it is our life's work to make sure that the world sees its light and feels its warmth.

Yes, Christ called Peter just as He calls the youth of today. His wanderings no longer take Him along the edge of the sea but into the schools and the drugstores. His call is the same. Follow Me! The invitation to pattern our life after His, to be His hands and His feet and His eyes; and it is an invitation that dare not be taken lightly. So we follow Him. We don't know exactly how; but we keep ourselves ready. And if He does not choose to send us out into the world to do great things for Him, then, little by little, the world will come to us, because the world will see in us something of Him who one day walked the highways of our earth.

2 THE WOMAN IN HIS LIFE

She must have been a terrific girl; otherwise, she would never have been chosen to be the Mother of God. Christ wasn't going to choose just anybody. He wasn't going to pick a wag or a lamebrain. He did not want the kind of girl whose only contribution to the world was her sex appeal. He was going to choose the greatest. The most.

The rest of us couldn't do this. We didn't have the chance to choose our mothers. We had to take what we got. This is a good system because we all know that the mother God picked for us turned out to be far better than we could ever have chosen ourselves (and it's the rare bird, indeed, who doesn't feel this way about his mother). But Christ could bide His time until the right one came along. Which is what He did. He waited. He waited thousands of years. Then she came. Christ took her right to His heart because through a unique privilege she was preserved from all sin.

It would not be stretching things too far to say that Christ chose Mary for other reasons, too, beautifully human reasons. He wanted to be the Son of Mary so that He would look like her. He wanted to walk the way she walked; to speak as she spoke. And when He went down the street beside her, He wanted people to stop short and point at Him with the striking discovery, "Why, He looks just like His mother."

Christ, however, was not so taken by the beauty of her body – physical beauty is such an unimportant thing, anyway, so passing, so deceptive, and sometimes dangerous – but He was entirely taken by the beauty of her soul. Mary's humility made the difference. This was the virtue that rocks all of us back on our heels. Of course, she was pure, but so were all the other maidens who lived with her in the Temple. There they spent their time keeping the linens in repair, praying and searching Sacred Scripture. Through their studies they knew that the coming of the Messias was at hand – those prophecies again. It was in the books. It was in the air.

And while all the other girls were praying for the singular privilege of being the Mother of God, Mary was off somewhere praying a different kind of prayer. Not that she would be the Mother of God; but that she would be the servant, the handmaid of the Mother of God. If this isn't humility, what is?

Mary must have been about fourteen or fifteen years old when things really began to happen. Probably she had already been espoused to Joseph, which is another way of saying that Joseph and Mary were engaged. Now the Annunciation takes place. Annunciation is a big word but it simply means that the Angel Gabriel visited Mary and brought the news that she was to be the Mother of God. And no angel ever did a better job than Gabriel. His wording of the message was a masterpiece. He had three things to do. He must catch her attention, announce God's choice of her as His Mother, and then win her consent.

He did not want to gamble on his angelic beauty capturing her attention. Knowing Mary's complete absorption in God, he was afraid that she might be unimpressed by the presence of a mere archangel. So he took no chances. He knew of only one thing that would astonish the very humble Mary. Praise. So he started by praising her, "Hail, full of grace." His plan worked; he captured her attention completely.

Quickly he followed with a hint of miraculous conception, "The Lord is with thee," and finally he indicated the blessings that were to follow, "Blessed art thou among women." Indeed, Gabriel took no chances. Then he continued, "Behold, thou shalt conceive and bring forth a Son. . . . He shall be great . . . and of His kingdom there shall be no end . . . for nothing shall be impossible with God."

Gabriel did his job well. Mary was overwhelmed. But she was also intelligent and practical. Reminding Gabriel that she was a virgin and intended to remain one, she asked how it would be possible for her to fulfill her vow of virginity to God and still be a mother. Gabriel explained that Mary was not to be involved in the normal procedure in having a child. Her conceiving the Son of God was to be unique, special, miraculous. "The Holy Ghost shall come upon thee and the power of the most High shall overshadow thee." So Mary consented. Complete surrender, complete dedication. "Behold the handmaid of the Lord; be it done to me according to thy word." And with this the course of the world was changed and the Son of God took flesh in Mary's womb.

She had been prepared for all this. It was not just a spur of the moment choice. When Mary was born, she received a privilege that had not been given to anyone else in the history of the world. The rest of us were born with the stain of original sin, that backwash of Adam's infidelity; but Mary was born completely free from all sin. This is why she is called the Immaculate Conception.

People are always getting this mixed up. The Immaculate Conception has nothing to do with the birth of Christ. It has nothing to do with the actual fact of a virgin giving birth to a child. The Immaculate Conception is not a statement of any kind of miraculous conception; it is simply a statement of the fact that Mary was preserved from all sin, and would forever remain so, from the very first moment of her life in the womb of her mother, St. Anne.

Shortly after the long talk with Gabriel, Mary decided to visit her cousin, Elizabeth, who was soon to become the mother of John the Baptist. Elizabeth lived up in the hill country of Judea, and up into the hills went Mary to see her. Elizabeth, in the meantime, has been told by an angel that Mary was to be the Mother of God. So when she saw Mary approach, she, being a rather excitable, vociferous person, went running to her doorstep, screaming, "Blessed art thou among women and blessed is the fruit of thy womb!"

But Mary, shunning notoriety and immune to flattery and praise, said softly, "Shhh! Someone might hear you," and then, by way of explanation, raised her voice in what we refer to today as her *Magnificat.*

"My soul magnifies the Lord . . . For, behold, henceforth all generations shall call me blessed; because he who is mighty has done great things for me. . . ."

This was Mary, the girl who recognized everything good in her as coming from God and who attributed nothing to herself – an outlook, a conviction that made her so different from the rest of us. So we, who are nothing, but think we are so great, might easily learn from the little maiden of Nazareth – who was truly great, but thought she was nothing.

3 ❦ FOR THIS DAY

Caesar Augustus, reclining on his sumptuous couch, flicked the remnants of honeyed locusts from his fingers and called to a servant for his map. It was unrolled before him – and how he loved to look at it! Emblazoned across the top were the glorious words: "Rome, Empire of the World" – and it was all his, his kingdom, with one official language, Latin, and one ruler, Caesar.

He wanted to know how many people he ruled. He wanted to know the extent of his power. He intended to bleed them for more taxes.

"How many subjects do I have?" he asked. Nobody seemed to know for certain. There were just too many to count. "Then we shall find out. We shall take a census of the world." So a decree went out to all the people within the reaches of Rome's screaming eagles. Caesar never realized it, but he was the one who raised the curtain on the final act of God's great plan for the redemption of mankind.

On the fringe of the empire in the little village of Nazareth, soldiers tacked upon the walls the order of Caesar requiring every citizen to register in the town of his ancestors. The people of Nazareth read it and grumbled, as they were always grumbling. The citizens of Nazareth were the dead-end kids of Palestine. They were brawlers who liked a good fight. They would steal the money out of a blind man's cup. So established and recognized was their reputation that if anybody dared call you a Nazarene, you went after him, fangs bared. It was one of the worst names to be called.

When the news spread around town, they cursed all the more. They cursed Rome. They cursed Caesar. They cursed the world and life in general. And probably, as the night wore on, they wondered in the backs of their wine-soaked minds, "Where is this Messias who is supposed to come and free us from the heavy hand of Rome?" But they knew they could not fight the city hall, so they finally staggered off to their homes and prepared to move.

For Joseph the decree solved a very thorny problem. By now he understood the condition of Mary; he knew that she was to become the Mother of God. But he also knew the prophecies. Five hundred years before, Micheas had prophesied: "Thou Bethlehem are the least of the cities of Juda and out of thee will He come forth who is to be a ruler in Israel" (5:2).

Joseph, living in Nazareth and not knowing just how he was going to get to Bethlehem, found, in the decree of Caesar, his reason for moving and the fulfillment of the prophecy. So he made some hurried preparations, assembled a few necessary things for the trip, fastened the front door, took Mary by the hand, and headed south. Probably they started out on foot, because an old legend tells us that along the way Joseph obtained a donkey to make traveling easier for Mary.

We who complain about smokey buses with square wheels and drafty trains with soot-lined window sills might profitably pause to check this journey that Mary and Joseph made down to Bethlehem. Today we all have gasoline feet; we travel by car on turnpikes. Seventy miles is a breeze. We can clock that in an hour. But these two went by foot; to make a trip like that in their time, under those circumstances, in four days, was like breaking the sound barrier. The seventy-mile trip took them a good five days.

First of all, at the time of year the weather was at its worst. True, there weren't any blizzards. Snow was a rarity, and when it fell it never lasted long. The temperature never went down to zero. The coldest it gets in that region is about 25 degrees, which is cold enough when you're out in the open all night.

The roads were horrible. They were not the fine, well-kept highways built by the Romans who were masters of the art. They were so poor that the caravans of camels and donkeys could barely manage them.

Time and again, Mary and Joseph were shoved off into the ditches while the lumbering caravans of the wealthier sons of David went tooling by. The traffic was frightening. The four or five stopovers required in the course of the journey were perhaps spent in the homes of friends, or more likely in the public inns where, with other travelers, they slept on the ground among the animals.

They made it, though. They reached Bethlehem. But

when they did, they found conditions even worse. The village was spilling over with people. What happened next is expressed in the saddest words ever written, "There was no room for them in the inn."

Oh, they could have found some corner in a crowded room. But Mary's time was near and what she wanted most of all was privacy. Joseph was on the spot. Wasn't there a private room somewhere? Of course there was, but he would have had to "grease a palm" to get one. "Slip me a five and you can have a room"—the old under-the-counter stuff. Nothing ever stopped money from talking, even in those days. If you had the "dough," you were in; if you didn't, you were out. It was as simple as that. A man's worth is usually measured by the "lettuce" in his wallet.

But Joseph had no money. He was broke. Most of it had probably gone to purchase the little donkey. So he turned away from the greedy keeper of the inn, walked back to where his lovely wife was waiting, took the bridle in his hand, and, wiping his sleeve across his eyes, started back down the hill into the darkness.

Just a little way out of town, a cave in a chalk hill opened upon the road. These were common in the area. Joseph turned and threw a questioning look at Mary. She rewarded him with a gentle smile and a barely perceptible nod of her head. They went in. The place was already partially occupied by animals; it was probably dark and filthy. But it was somewhat removed from the village and therefore quiet and private, and that was enough for this expectant mother. Mary knelt to pray when Joseph set to work. He hung his lantern on the damp wall and prepared one corner in the place that seemed more comfortable and less dirty. He made a bed of clean straw, unpacked the knapsack, and settled down.

This was the place that God, from all eternity, had chosen as the birthplace of His only Son; and there, in the dim light, the Nativity came to pass.

There was no noise. Bethlehem was crowded, but nobody knew what had transpired in the cave. Jerusalem was only five miles away, but nobody knew there, either. It was all so quiet. No one was there to welcome Christ. "He came unto His own and His own received Him not." No confusion, no revelry, no clamor of His subjects. Only silence. A silence that was broken only by the sound of water dripping down the side of the cave and the soft, muffled snorting of animals.

Outside, angels carried the message on the winds to the shepherds. "Do not be afraid . . . for today in the town of David a Saviour has been born to you, who is Christ the Lord."

The birth of Christ certainly changed our lives. Because of His coming to earth, our nature has been elevated, ennobled, almost deified, making us sort of blood relations of God. We have received supernatural life, grace, and glory. It makes God somewhat like us; it makes us somewhat like God.

The birth of Christ proved many things: that there is nothing wrong with poverty, nothing shameful about it; and that there is nothing right about pride. The Greek philosophers were never invited to His crib; neither were the Scribes, the Pharisees, nor the Roman tyrants. The only people who were invited were the kind of people who stooped low to enter the cave. For only those who are willing to stoop lowly before the King are worthy to stand proudly beside His throne.

4 A MAN WITH TROUBLES

St. Joseph was a man who never knew what trouble was until he got married. We don't know much about him, but what we do know comes to us from the Gospel of St. Matthew.

Luke was a ladies' man. His Gospel is filled with the accounts of women who crossed the path of Christ. But he was a doctor with a waiting room constantly filled with women. He just couldn't get away from them. Matthew, on the other hand, was a man's man. He was a man of the street. As a tax collector, he dealt with men almost exclusively. He transacted business with all types of them – the wheat tycoons, the big oil merchants, small businessmen, and laborers – everybody had to pay taxes, then as today.

He was a "shrewdie" all right. In his racket he had to be. He could measure men. The big hello, the clap on the back, the wide smile – all surface nonsense. He could see beneath the surface. He could spot the "phony." But he could also case people well enough to know when the genuine article came along.

That is why he was so impressed by this man Joseph. That is why he wrote about him. Probably Joseph and Matthew had never met, but that didn't matter. Matthew knew him. He wanted the world to know him, too. Nobody else had anything to say about the foster father of Christ. Not that he was deliberately rejected. Not that his family or friends had any reason to be ashamed of him. It was just that he traveled in big company. He was lost in the shadows. And again, recorders of history passed him over because he never did anything that might make good copy in the press. There was nothing notorious about him. Nothing spectacular.

But the little we know about him is quite enough. A doggedness, a humility, an unquestioned devotion to his family marked all his life. He had his worries, too. He worried about Mary's condition when they made that hard trip to Bethlehem. And when they got there, he suffered the shock of being turned away from the inns because there was no room. There was the panicky search for quarters of some kind.

Then the flight into Egypt with Herod's baby killers hot on his trail. And through his whole life the drudgery of the carpenter shop in which he earned a livelihood for his wife and child, all the time wishing, in a very human way, that he were able to do more, even to the laying of diamonds and priceless fabrics at the feet of his wife.

No, he never really knew trouble until he married Mary. Before then he worked hard and well at his trade, well off the beaten track of civilization.

He was known among his neighbors as a "just man," which was just about the best thing that anybody could have said about you in those days. Being a just man meant there was nothing wrong with you. He was just plain good, a real straight-shooter. He faithfully observed all the laws. Religion to him was not just a lot of lip service. He did not just talk it. He lived it. It was the very warp and woof of his whole existence.

You can still see the type in the parishes today. The same kind of prudent, conscientious, noble Catholic father or young man who quietly and without publicity lives his life and does his duty. It's the best kind you can get.

So Joseph lived in serene, uneventful peace. Nothing out of the ordinary ever happened to him. His was the quiet routine of daily labor. He was not the old man with the long white beard, as he is sometimes pictured, but the fine, strong youth, biding his time, waiting for his hour when the will of God would show itself to him.

Then she came into his life. We don't know under what circumstances they met. But their families got together and decided that it would make a good match. Joseph went along with it. And when he did, when he was espoused to Mary, the tempo of his life picked right up. All of a sudden he was confused. His wife was with child, something he could not understand since they were living as brother and sister. He found himself being shaken awake in the middle of the night by no less than an angel of the Lord with a command to leave town. Some crazy king was trying to kill the Infant Jesus. So he went all the way into Egypt where conditions were not so hot. By now his head was spinning. How would he get a job in a foreign land when he didn't even know the language?

Yes, Mary brought trouble into Joseph's life. But strangely enough, he loved every minute of it. He thrilled at the thought that he had been chosen to protect her. He never quite got over it. So he didn't quibble or complain. He didn't ask for a lot of silly explanations. He never questioned anything. He just did his duty. And why? The reason is obvious. It was very simple. Joseph, the carpenter, was in love.

It was this love that made him shoulder the responsibilities of his calling. And when you take a good look at Joseph, you find a "little" man who took over a big job. He didn't have any special training for it. He saw what had to be done, then went ahead and did it. No one else was chosen to shield this beautiful lady and her Child. He was. So he would shield them. He was the least of them, but he would be their leader. He would rise to the occasion. With God's help he would not "pass the buck" to others who, he thought, might do a better job. Because it wasn't a task for other people. It was for him.

And what a job he did! Shortly after the birth of Christ, he probably found a home in Bethlehem. Here he performed the rite of circumcision, by which Christ was enrolled among the Jews. Just as Baptism makes us Christians, circumcision set the Jews apart as God's chosen people. Certainly circumcision wasn't necessary for Christ, but Joseph was a stickler for the law. He always set the example for the rest of his family. So he also made sure that Mary fulfilled the Jewish law regarding mothers who had recently given birth to a child. It resembled our present-day ceremony of the churching of women. Forty days after giving birth to a child, the mother was expected to be at the Temple for purification. It was the law. So Joseph made sure that Mary was there, even though it was not necessary for her to take part in it.

It is true that Christ had no human father, but His foster father, His protector, Joseph, cared for Him and His Mother as if they were his very own. Joseph was always their beacon. He possessed all the qualities of a good husband and good father. He was a prudent man, knowing when to speak and when to keep his mouth shut. He was a considerate man, knowing when he should be with Mary and Jesus, and when he should slip back into his shop. He was obedient. Whether it was the book of the law or the nocturnal command of an angel, he never questioned, but only obeyed. He was, as we have said, the very quintessence of manliness because he was looked upon by all as a "just man."

If Joseph lived in our times and went to our schools, you would never find him standing in the corridors, hands in his pockets, with a bored, cynical look on his face, as if the whole business of school were, after all, a bit childish and immature. He would have looked about, have seen what was expected of him, and then tackled it. He certainly would never have said, "Leave it to George to do."

He must have questioned his abilities many times. He must have shivered at the very idea of bringing up a Child who was the Son of God. But he did his duty and left us with a good thought. The best thing that any young man can do is to do what is expected of him.

5 CHRIST THE TEEN-AGER

The Magi were not so stupid. They were not going back to Herod and blab about the new King they had found in Bethlehem. They were wise to Herod; they didn't like the smell of things, so they slipped back to their country by another route.

When Herod realized that those kings from the East had pulled a fast one on him, he "blew his stack." If he couldn't find anybody to help him wipe out this little Interloper, this new threat to his throne, then he would do it himself. So, in a diabolic rage, he turned his soldiers loose with orders to go over to Bethlehem and put to the sword every boy under two years of age.

His orders were carried out. It wasn't much of a job; the

population of Bethlehem was only about 2000. And if you have only 2000 persons living in a town, you're not going to have very many kids under two crawling around. Therefore, we can figure that about 20 or 30 infants shed their blood for Christ. Certainly, there would not have been any more than that. They were the first martyrs of Christian times. They are called the Holy Innocents and their feast is celebrated on December 28.

While the blood was flowing, St. Joseph, having received another heavenly tip, was off and running. He was not on the main route to Egypt, either. It would have been more dangerous. Herod's soldiers would have nailed him before he reached the border. So he led Mary and the Child into Egypt the hard way – right out across the desert.

The journey was murder. In 55 B.C. the Roman army made the same crossing and it feared the trip more than it feared the war waiting in Egypt. Now the three travelers made it alone, dragging themselves laboriously over the shifting sands in the exhausting heat by day, spending the nights on the ground, sustaining themselves with the little food and water they could carry. Seven days later, tired but safe, they arrived in the town of Memphis, Egypt.

Anti-Semitism was running high in Egypt at that time. In spite of it, Joseph found friends there, other Jews who, like himself, had been forced to flee the wrath of Herod. Jews have always been in trouble; it is no exaggeration to say that the Jewish race has been the most persecuted in the history of the world. All through the centuries they have been running. Just as they ran from the Pharaoh with Moses at their head, so in our own time they ran from Hitler. And those who didn't run died. Joseph made his way to the ghetto, settled there, and found among his own people the companionship and the help he needed.

The Holy Family must have spent two years in Egypt. Then Herod, his stomach horribly ulcerated and writhing in convulsions, took his last breath, turned up his toes, and died. The news of his death was passed on to Joseph by an angel (those angels kept Joseph very, very busy), so he packed his belongings and said to Mary, "Let's go home."

His intention, of course, was to establish himself, his family, and his business in Bethlehem. Heaven knows, Bethlehem needed new inns and he was the man to help build them. But in the course of his preparations he learned that Archelaus, the son of Herod, was ruling over that area, and Archelaus was every bit as mean as his dad. So he decided, instead, to reside in Nazareth. Antipas was ruler there.

Right here, all of a sudden, Scripture clams up. Very little is said about the activities of the Holy Family from here on. Small wonder, then, that this period, lasting about thirty years, has always been called the Hidden Life.

In the first place, the physician evangelist Luke states that when the three settled in Nazareth, "the child grew, and became strong . . . full of wisdom, and the grace of God was upon Him." Shortly afterward, as if to point out that this continued, he repeats that at the age of twelve, Jesus was advancing "in wisdom and age and grace before God and men."

When He learned to toddle, He followed His Mother around the house and sang with her at her work. He played with chips of wood and little boats that Joseph had carved for Him. Yes, He was normal in a manner of speaking; but His senses were sharpened to the finest perfection. His vision, His sense of smell, His hearing; all these things were far superior to anybody else's. And with them, He observed things. All the examples that He used later in teaching His parables were taken, firsthand, from the people and the country around Him.

He dressed the same as the other neighborhood kids, in a red gown fastened at the waist by a brightly colored sash, with a jacket of white or blue. Without having to resort to barbells, He was in top physical shape all His life. As a boy, nobody kicked sand in His face down on the beach. He was never afraid to climb the heights, especially the blunt shoulders of Mount Thabor only five and a half miles from town. He wasn't afraid to descend into the hillside caverns. He could shout as loud as the next fellow and laugh as gleefully. Whatever kind of ball game they played, He was in on it. In their track meets He was a better sprinter than the rest of them. They didn't have air rifles, but Jesus knew how to handle a slingshot in expert fashion.

But no matter what He did, He was never known to snivel, accuse, cry, or run off at the mouth. He had no taste for triumph. If one thing set Him apart from His buddies, it was His lack of interest in the rewards of competition. He liked to run, but He cared nothing for the prize. He would contend in boyish trials of strength, but never took pleasure in lording it over His defeated partner. He never tried to be a "big operator." He never had to resort to His divine powers to impress His friends. He never felt the need to employ miracles in order to make Himself the center of attention.

He was obedient to His parents. He never gave His parents any lip. When they sent Him to the store, He went happily. When they told Him what time to be in at night, He was in. He respected the judgments of Mary and Joseph, because, being adults, they had experience. He could have swung the whole world like a trinket on a string, but when His parents spoke, He listened.

He went along with the strict rules of family life. The Holy Family, like all the other neighbors, would rather have been stoned to death than break any of the laws. And the laws were tough. On the Sabbath, for instance, no one could light a fire or put one out. A man could not peel a piece of fruit. A woman could not knead dough. A boy could not wash his dog. A girl could not plait her hair. An old man could not tie a knot in a string. No one could write, or cross out what had been written. And Jesus obeyed because of His intense respect of the Law.

His early education came from His Mother, but later He went to the village school. His friends, naturally, dreaded the whole idea of school, but boys in Nazareth had to go whether they liked it or not. Nearly 2000 years ago education in that hillside town was compulsory, and there was a Nazareth school board that saw to it that no child played hookey after he was six years old. Christ went along with all this.

Yes, Scripture is very silent about the boyhood of Christ. The Child who held the thread while His Mother was spinning – was God. The Boy who sped gaily on an errand at her request – was God. It was God who dutifully worked the hammer and saw, under Joseph's direction. And there was nothing in the way of a big production in His doing it. He was a perfect Son to His parents, who, without saying a word, taught one of His greatest lessons; even the Son of God saw the wisdom and safety in obedience to His parents.

6 HIS FATHER'S BUSINESS

Just as soon as my mother recovered from the shock of my arrival, she got busy with her pen and sent out word to all her family and friends that she had just given birth to her third son. And to hear my father, you might have believed that *he* had given birth to me. Quite a lot of people knew about me when I was born. They all came over to huddle around my crib and see the eighth wonder of the world.

Even Christ didn't get as much attention. As an Infant He was recognized only three times for what He really was. The unimportant people of the world, the shepherds, tracked mud into the cave and fell to their knees in adoration of Him.

Then the important people of the world, the Magi, arrived in worldly magnificence to lay treasures at His feet.

Finally, Simeon, the old man of Candlemas, recognized Christ. He was standing in the Temple – waiting. When the inconspicuous young couple with their Baby came in, the long-awaited jolt went through Simeon; and with the bounce of youth, he hurried over to look into the rosy, little face, to take the King into his arms, and to gasp softly in so many words, "This is it. Now I've had it. Now I'm ready to check out."

Simeon, the Magi, the Shepherds – the big three, the people who recognized Christ when He came to earth. For these people the flame of God's presence burst before them. And we are enjoying this. So we settle back to watch the shock, the joy, the thrill of all the others to whom He will reveal Himself. But we are disappointed because now Christ goes into hiding, makes Himself unknown to men, effaces Himself so completely that in later life when He begins His public ministry as teacher and worker of miracles, all His neighbors are so surprised that they repeatedly ask one another, "Is this not the carpenter?"

We don't like to see Him hide, but we can't do anything about it. We can only resign ourselves and patiently stand by until the day when He will come forth to make Himself known to the people of His village, to the sick and the crippled, the deaf, dumb, and blind, and to the smug Pharisees up in Jerusalem.

But Christ fools us. We are willing to wait for Him, mind you, until He begins His public life, but just about halfway between His infancy and His adulthood, He decided to put in an appearance. St. Luke tells us of it.

According to Mosaic law, a boy became a man at the age of 12. When our Saviour became officially a man, He subjected Himself to all the requirements of the law. Among other things, He was expected to join the Jewish men in their annual pilgrimage to Jerusalem for the feast of the Pasch. Really, it was for men only; but you could not keep the women away. Men in front, the women brought up the rear. And how they enjoyed the trip. The pilgrims loved it because it was the commemoration of their deliverance from the land of bondage, Egypt. The priests welcomed it because it meant added shekels in the Temple coffers – and in their own pockets. The concessioners loved it. They did a record business in their souvenir stores and in whatever they had in place of hot-dog stands.

It was the event of the year. We have our Labor Day week ends and our Memorial Day week ends when everybody hits the road and many of them never come back, having taken the modern way into eternity – behind the wheel. This pilgrimage was the Labor-Memorial Day of the Jewish people. Weeks before the roads were graded to make them more passable; bridges were reinforced to hold up under the added burdens of a million feet; tombstones were whitewashed or fenced in to prevent their being touched by an occasional stray. If you touched a tombstone, in those days, you were outside the law, unclean.

Several million persons gathered in and around Jerusalem for the feast. The whole celebration lasted a week. First, there was the solemn eating of the paschal lamb. The following day, special sacrifices were offered, ending with a ceremony where a paste, made of flour and oil, was burned upon the altars of holocaust.

At the end of the week, everybody started back. It was a mess, an undisciplined mob of men, women, and screaming children; deafening shouts of persons calling and looking for one another; beasts of burden trampling food and kicking over water buckets.

It's no wonder Mary and Joseph got their signals crossed. On the first day out, Mary thought Jesus was with Joseph, and Joseph thought He was with Mary. That night they found out how wrong they were. Many children were missing because they always get lost in crowds. The difference with the missing Christ was that He didn't get lost at all. He slipped away from His parents on important business of His own. He simply ducked out on them.

Being badly shaken up, Mary and Joseph started back over the ten miles they had just covered that day. They found Him – three days later. There He was in the Temple, sitting in the midst of the doctors, engaged in a very lively and intelligent discussion – we don't know just what about. It would be nice if Luke had told us what He was saying to these men, but Luke didn't tell us and that is that.

If anyone ever mentions apocryphal writings, you can be sure they are about as genuine as an eight-dollar bill. Among this collection of bogus history, there is the so-called Gospel of St. Thomas which unscrupulously and boldly tells us that at this particular time, the Boy Jesus was explaining to the rabbis the mysteries of the heavenly bodies – how many there were, their nature, and their movement – plus a few facts about physics, metaphysics, hyperphysics, hypophysics, and a dozen other things. All of which is utterly preposterous.

If anything, Christ was throwing "loaded" questions at them, triggering their minds in the hope that they might, in the light of His pure logic, slowly perceive that the time of His coming, as mentioned by the prophets, was indeed at hand.

St. Luke tells us that when Mary and Joseph saw Him there, "they wondered." Indeed, they must have. Mary wondered why He had run out on them. Joseph wondered – his feet smarting from all this walking – how he might scold the Child, in the light of His divinity. They called Him from His engaging conversation and asked with marked disappointment, "Why hast Thou done this to us?"

So He gave them the answer. He told them, "How is it that you sought Me? Did you not know that I must be about My Father's business?"

Mary and Joseph did not understand. But we can. Already the Redeemer was at work. He was revealing, however gradually, to these intellectuals that He was ready. He would spend most of His public life with the poor and the ignorant; but because He loved all men and was sent to save all men, He was there in the Temple, throwing His bombs in the midst of the intelligent and educated. No one would be excluded from His kingdom.

The consoling thing about all this is that He was about His Father's business; and His Father's business was then, still is, and always will be – YOU!

7 IN TRAINING

It takes about four years to run a four-minute mile – not four minutes. Training, you know. And if a golfer wants to win a National Open, it will take more than 263 strokes. About 263,000 would be more like it. Again it is a question of training.

Nobody ever did anything worthwhile on the spur of the moment. Glory or success comes only after years of work and planning. And if this applies to relatively minor things like track meets and golf tournaments, then it certainly applies to Christ who was faced with the biggest job that was ever handed out to anyone – the salvation of the world. His mission on earth was to lift the human race up from its dark squalor, a task of no small proportions. He had a job to do. Naturally it took preparation – lots of it.

So, after His brief appearance in the pages of St. Luke when up in the Temple, by the force of His intelligence and His logic, He left the rabbis talking to themselves, He went back home with His folks, and the curtains closed again. Probably the learned men in the Temple expected this brilliant Boy with the searching mind to return. But He didn't. Soon they forgot about Him, and never knew how close they had come to touching God.

He was too busy getting ready down in Nazareth. For eighteen years more He would live there, completely isolated from the world at large.

Sometime during these years Joseph died, but we don't know when. Mary's parents, Joachim and Anna, also went to the bosom of Abraham, the Jewish expression for heaven. Jesus went on with His preparations.

First of all, He decided to learn, in an experimental, human way, all the things He already knew by virtue of His divinity. He didn't *have* to do this because He possessed divine knowledge, beatific knowledge, and infused knowledge. One thing He did *not need* was an education. But because he was a perfect man, He thought it would be wise to learn things progressively like other men. Further, normal occupation with learning would preserve the secrecy of His divine mission.

Therefore, He picked up reading, writing, and arithmetic at the village school. He knew Aramaic because that was the language spoken then. But He also studied and mastered Hebrew, which at that time was a dead language, much as Latin is today. He knew Greek.

His specialty, of course, was the study of the Bible. In addition to hearing it read publicly in the synagogue on Saturdays, He read it privately. He set us a good example here. The Bible is the best selling book in the world – there are millions of them around – but not enough people pick them up. Nor did Christ find the Old Testament conveniently bound in leather as it is for us. The best He could do was borrow portions of it from the chief of the synagogue.

But He knew the Bible. And when later in His preaching He used words such as, "Have you not read?" "What is written in the law?" "How readest thou?" He knew what He was talking about. He fed His mind on the Bible. No one ever interpreted it with greater clearness, depth, or authority. He especially loved to quote the Psalms and the prophets.

He learned other things in other ways. He kept his eyes open. He observed. He wasn't just down here to kill time. He watched closely the domestic, political, and social life going on around Him at all times. He interested Himself in everything.

Nature was also His teacher. He constantly beheld around Him in nature the hand marks of His heavenly Father. Later, while preaching in parables, He disclosed His lifelong attentiveness to the seemingly most insignificant details of life and nature. The lily of the field, the growing wheat, the cockle sowed by enemies, the fig tree with leaves but no fruit, the vine that must be pruned to bear more fruit, the birds of the air, the hen gathering her chicks under her wings, the sheep following the shepherd, the sunset, the burning south wind, the lake, the mountains, and a hundred other features – He knew them all and He loved them.

Using His eyes further, He learned many other things. What He saw in Nazareth was but a miniature of vast poverty, bewilderment, and oppression. He was the solitary figure in a boisterous town who saw clearly the people being taken in by their leaders, robbed blind by thieves in high places, and bossed around by superstitious old men who split hairs over rules and regulations. Yes, it taught Him to realize that the day must come for Him to drop His tools, leave His home and His mother, and devote the remainder of His life to bringing light and comfort to the lost and frightened. But He had to be ready. He had to continue developing Himself, physically, intellectually, and spiritually.

His training in the carpenter shop continued. Labor had always been despised and shunned, but He consecrated labor by the touch of His hand to a tool. This was the way He would support Mary when Joseph died. Christ was not going to be a free-loader.

But that phase of His life which really made Him an educated man was His practice of prayer. Without prayer, He knew His work could never be done. In His capacity as man, He perceived the utter futility and the folly of trying to live or trying to do anything without first getting on His knees. He was going to make it an essential of the spiritual life; so He prayed. And constantly.

We have no record of how He addressed His Father during these years, but it is enough for us to know that He prayed. He spent thirty years in prayer before He dared open His mouth in public, while some of us have the gall to think that we can go ahead and accomplish something good without first asking God for assistance. It's ridiculous. He spent thirty years prayerfully preparing for three; and in His public life, He never did anything without first asking His Father's help. Before He chose His Apostles, He prayed; and sometimes He spent the whole night at it. Before His Transfiguration, He took Peter, James, and John and went up into the mountains to pray. Before He multiplied the loaves and fishes, at the grave of Lazarus, at the Last Supper, in His final agony – always prayer.

His youth was not a wasted span of years, not a long period of stagnation, not a mere existence or passage of time. He used His youth to prepare for His manhood. Fortifying Himself in every way, He was able to measure up to the great battle. Concentrated effort it took, attention to the important things, cultivation of the best habits; then He was ready.

So the matured Jesus, now thirty years old and brooding over the tribulations of the world, was ready to offer it joy. A new way of life and not a dreary servitude – this was His gift to the world. All that men and women of good will had ever hoped for and dreamed of was about to come true. In the high hills around His home, Jesus, the Workman, made Himself ready to do what He had come to do. Now His heart was burning with a new, dynamic message. He had reached manhood; His hair was long and soft and golden brown. He had His Mother's glorious dark eyes; His muscles were strong and hard from labor.

Then, on a certain day, strange word trickled into Nazareth, word of a strong man from Judea's wilderness, a man who preached in various towns down south, blessing people with the waters of the river Jordan; a new man named John.

John the Baptist, they called him. He was telling great crowds that he was only the herald, the forerunner, preparing a reception for the Saviour of the world and leaving a message. The message? It was simple. "Prepare. The Messias is coming at last!"

8 RECRUITING HIS ARMY

When Jesus bade a tearful good-by to His Mother and started out on the open road to fulfill His destiny, He was the great Captain ready for battle, but He was not the man of the hour. St. John the Baptist was. The Baptist was the talk of the town, the conversation piece around every table, the big scoop of the year. Crowds followed him everywhere and Jesus followed the crowds. He wanted to get a look at this cousin of His whom He had never seen before.

John had gained his reputation by erupting upon the pages of history like a roaring volcano. He had spent his lifetime alone, isolated in the desert, out of step with the times – and he looked it. He had never been to a barber; his hair was long and shaggy. He wore a cloak of camel's hair with a leather belt around his waist. And, no matter how you say it, he was skinny, because nobody can eat locusts and wild honey over a period of fifteen or twenty years and still be fat, or even healthy. He was a fearless, fiery apparition just in from the desert. He had a singular purpose: to preach penance to the Jews so that they might be ready to receive the Messias.

John spared no one with his scathing words, neither big nor little people. He aimed his vocal guns at the Pharisees, those hypocrites who kept the laws externally but were rotten underneath. He scorched the Sadducees, the materialists who were so broadminded that they favored rejecting the old Jewish beliefs and taking on the paganism of Rome because of political ambition. John raked the Publicans over the coals because of their dishonesty and their avarice in the tax-collecting business. He blistered them all and lumped them under one heading, "brood of vipers."

Yet, John the Baptist was not to become famous solely because of his violent tirades against sin and sensuality. John was destined to be the last of the prophets of the Old Law and was to prefigure, in his baptizing of Christ, the Sacrament of Baptism.

When we read of John's baptizing in the river Jordan, we have here nothing new but only a revival of an ancient Jewish custom. Baptism, as we have it today, is a sacrament instituted by Christ that carries grace with it. John's baptism did not give grace because it was not yet a sacrament. All it was, actually, was a "washing" or an external cleansing of the body representing the cleansing of the soul. It was only a type of that Sacrament which was later to be instituted by Christ; for without Christ there would be no sacraments. What John's baptism could do, and did, was to prepare men for Christ and a worthy reception of His Sacrament, by leading them to penance and accustoming them to that ceremony which Christ was to make an absolute requisite for admission into heaven.

So one day when John was preaching to the crowds, "Repent, for the kingdom of heaven is at hand," he looked out and saw the Stranger. They had never met before, but John knew Jesus when he saw Him. Jesus asked if He, too, could be baptized. John, hulking, vociferous, sweating with earnestness, answered in unbelief, "But it is I who ought to be baptized by Thee." Christ smiled and replied, "Let it be so now, for so it becomes us to fulfill all justice."

Here was the world's greatest show of humility. John, his wild head bowed – that same head which soon was to be severed at the request of a dancer – presuming to purify by water the Saviour of the world; and Christ, the Son of God, submitting to this cleansing as if He were a sinner. It was all too spectacular. The two cousins walked from the shore into the tumbling Jordan River.

After the ceremony was completed and they had returned to the shore, the heavens opened and Christ saw a vision of the Holy Spirit descending upon Him in the form of a dove, and a voice of the Father, saying, "Thou art my beloved Son; in Thee I am well pleased." This was the first occasion in the Gospels when the mystery of the Blessed Trinity was revealed – the Father in the voice from heaven, the Holy Spirit appearing as a dove, and the Son present in the person of Jesus.

At this moment, the inactive stage of Christ's life came to an end. No longer was He the contemplative wrapped within Himself and cut off from the world, but the soldier girded for war. It was the beginning of the positive work of redemption and the Holy Trinity was witness to it. Here God solemnly presented His Son to the world as its Redeemer.

Then John slips back into the shadows, deliberately, for, as he said, "Christ must increase while I must decrease." The Master proceeds to recruit followers and His choice falls on every man. Andrew and John were first. Then Andrew brought his brother Simon. Simon went to the hut where Jesus was and entered. Christ said to him, "Thou art Simon, the son of John; thou shalt be called Cephas." This was the Aramaic name for "rock." Peter is the Greek word for "rock." So what Christ really said to him was, "You will be called Rock." He gave Simon a name which He explained later, when He announced that He would build His Church upon Peter, the Rock.

Philip, a humble lad and friend of John, joined the group

9 WAR IN THE DESERT

One of Satan's biggest jobs in the world today is trying to make people believe that he does not exist. And when people emphatically deny the existence of a devil, they play right into his hands. An invisible person can get about better and accomplish more than a visible person; and the devil, the father of lies, is invisible.

Satan does not have any trouble with the souls who do not believe in him, for they already belong to him. They are his. But he is unsettled by those who know all about him. For these, he needs all his reinforcements. Satan must keep thousands of devils stationed at convent walls, but he alone can adequately patrol the corridors of the Kremlin. His work there is done. And if there is anyone in all the world who thinks himself so good as to be beyond the reach of Satan, he need only open the Bible to the desert scene.

After Christ had been baptized by John in the Jordan, He took the road to Jerusalem. It was wintertime and the empty skies and dreary desert were to form the background for His first real encounter with Satan. St. Mark says, "Now the spirit drove Him forth into the desert. And He was in the desert forty days and forty nights, being tempted the while by Satan."

If you can believe in George Washington because you read about him in some reliable history book, then you can believe in Christ and Satan because the Bible does not dish up lies for our consumption. Christ went into the desert to prepare Himself, by prayer and fasting, for the work ahead of Him. Toward the end of His long fast, Satan made his first overture toward the Son of God. Indeed, Satan was a bit uneasy about Christ. Was this the Messias or not? Satan had observed Christ's remarkable holiness. Was this really the Son of God? He was not sure.

Satan took into hell the same intellect he possessed as an archangel, but there was much he could not understand about the Incarnation. The self-control and the perfect bearing of this Man baffled him. He must find out. So as Christ approached the end of His long fast, Satan resolved to take advantage of His fatigue. Christ, burdened by the weight of the world's sins and having been without food for so long, was enduring a veritable torture. So Satan, taking some visible but not hideous form, approached Jesus to tempt Him.

Ordinarily, the temptations of man fall into three categories. They are temptations of the flesh (lust), or of the mind (pride), or of things (avarice). In his youth a person is more often tempted against purity and inclined toward the sins of the flesh. In middle age he is more likely to be tempted in his mind through pride and hunger for power. But as he reaches old age, his temptations are centered around avarice and the possession of worldly things. But whatever temptation he must endure, man takes three steps to it. First, suggestion: the evil is presented in an attractive light. Second, pleasure: the evil becomes a source of delight. Third, consent: the evil present is chosen by the will.

The human flesh that Christ had taken upon Himself was not for leisure but for battle. Satan saw in Christ an extraordinary human being whom he suspected of being the Messias. If he had known for sure, he might just as well have saved himself the trouble. But he did not know. That is why, in tempting Jesus, he always prefixed his statements with the word, "If."

There were three distinct types of temptation here. There is an old, old saying that the best way to a man's heart is through his stomach. This is the technique Satan used in his first temptation. He knew that Christ was hungry, so the devil pointed down at the little black stones that actually looked like glazed loaves of bread, fragments of hard pyrites polished by wind into roundish shapes with bright luster, and said, "If Thou art the Son of God, command that these stones become loaves of bread." Yes, the devil was clever. Christ had been without a bite of food for over a month. He was starving. But with complete assurance, He answered, "Not by bread alone does man live, but by every word that comes forth from the mouth of God."

Here, in His answer to Satan, Christ does not deny the need for food, but He does give it its proper place. In so many words He says to the devil, "You are tempting Me away from My cross. You want me to do battle with a full stomach. You want Me to choose outer abundance rather than inner holiness. I am hungry indeed, but My stomach groans so that the starving, crawling wrecks of humanity will never be able to say that God does not know what hunger is."

Satan lost his round. He could not draw our Lord away from His cross by offering bread, so he would try another approach. He now tempted Christ to pride and egotism. The devil raised Him to a lofty pinnacle of the temple and said, "Throw Thyself down; for it is written, 'He will give His angels charge concerning Thee.'" What the devil is saying here is: "Don't take the long hard way around. Take a short cut. Be a magician. The people are bored. Their life is a monotony. Show them something they will never forget. Put on a big show."

The answer of Christ, "Thou shalt not tempt the Lord thy God," means: "I refuse to perform stunts to win souls. It is only when I am lifted up on My cross that I will draw the world to Me. I will win followers not by My tricks but by My blood."

The devil's third attempt was the only one left. He could not tempt Christ through His body by bread. He could not tempt Him through His spirit by pride. So he tried to pierce the armor of Christ by appealing to His love for power. Satan here used the most frightening words in Scripture. Referring to the kingdoms of earth, he said, "To me they have been delivered, and to whomever I will give them. Therefore if thou wilt worship before me, the whole shall be thine." His language was really modern there. "I'm running this world," the devil said. "Thirty-seven out of every one hundred persons are in slavery. Adore me and I will cut You in on it. No sweat, no pain, no cross. Just get on Your knees before me and I will give it to You. It is mine to give."

But the Saviour of the world, knowing that His kingdom could be won only by His suffering and death, cut off the proud boasting of Satan. The majesty of divine command was in His voice when He dismissed the demon, saying, "Begone Satan, for it is written, 'The Lord thy God shalt thou worship and Him only shalt thou serve.'"

The ordeal was over. Christ had survived the wildest onslaughts of Satan. He left the desert. Then the reasons for it all were clear. He let Himself be tempted to teach us that nobody escapes temptation. He merited for us the grace to rise above all temptation. And He showed us how to contend with it when it comes. The difference between Christ and ourselves is this: He had no weaknesses. We do. There was no possibility of His succumbing to the wiles of Satan, but there is every possibility of our succumbing. Youth is threatened with many temptations every day. There is no reason to be afraid of the setup. There is certainly no reason for surprise. Everybody feels the hot breath of Satan, even the best of souls. No class, no nationality, no group, no individual is beyond the reach of Satan.

But Christ revealed the thin skin of Satan. He was able to stand and slug it out with hell. And He was victorious. We can always be victorious, too. We don't have to stand and fight as He did. We just aren't that big or that powerful. But we are all good runners, and there is nothing wrong with running. Because no matter how you look at it, whether you think it is a weakness to run or not, one thing is certain – when you run away from Satan, you automatically run right into the arms of Christ!

10 CANA

After Jesus had successfully cut Satan down to size in the desert, He made the rounds, lining up His Apostles for the big push. But before He could lead them into Jerusalem, something else came up. He found Himself with a wedding invitation. The newlyweds-to-be were probably good friends of His Mother, and Mary had sent word to Him, somehow, to be there. He was still the dutiful and obedient Son; if Mary said to show up for the wedding, that is exactly what He was going to do.

A wedding today is another of those things that keep us in constant movement; but in the old days, a wedding was a very special occasion that offered a rare break in routine living. It was not just a family affair; it was tribal.

The custom of the time required a wedding feast to last seven days, if the bride was being married for the first time; three days if the bride was a widow. The most popular month for a wedding was March, the time of the year in Palestine when nature was awakening and the farmers had a good deal of leisure. Custom set Wednesday for the beginning of the celebration, probably because it was as far away from the Sabbath as possible. On Tuesday evening the girl's relatives started getting her spruced up for the wedding, a task of no small proportions since bridal attire consisted of twenty-four different articles. She wore a crown on her head, rings and bracelets on her hands and feet, and a necklace. Then came the cosmetics – cheeks and lips tinted red, fingernails and hair tinted gold, eyelids touched with a feminine something which made her eyes seem large and more brilliant.

As dusk fell, the groom came with his companions to seek her. It was the most solemn moment of the feast and the whole village took part in it; even the strictest rabbis had to interrupt their studies to join the procession. Then after the ritual vase had been broken and the oaths exchanged, the party began.

The Jews, ordinarily abstemious people, really put on a meal at a time like this. Meat, game, and stuffed fish followed each other in a constant stream, all strongly flavored with onion. Mutton stew with milk was the perennial favorite. There were fresh vegetables and dried fruits. But the highlight of the bill of fare, the success of the whole wedding, rested on the quality of the wine that was served. A wedding feast without good wine was preposterous, and the wines of Palestine have always been excellent.

This wedding feast was nicely under way . . . when tragedy struck! The supply of wine went low. Just why this happened is not clear. It could not have been that the newlyweds were financially embarrassed; you just didn't shave expenses on your wedding day. Probably it was because Christ and His Apostles were there – and their attendance attracted many uninvited guests. At any rate, the host of the party was destined for supreme embarrassment – unless something could be done about it. It was Mary who, noticing the situation, set out to do something.

She approached Jesus and simply said, "They have no wine." His answer seems like something of a rebuff to His Mother. Indeed, it sounds off key in English; but in Aramaic it was quite proper and respectful. First of all, He used the term, "Woman," which in His own language was a salutation of the highest courtesy. Then He went on, "What wouldst thou have Me do? My Hour has not yet come." What it really meant in the jargon of our day was: "Mother, I would do anything in the world for you, and you know it. We have been living in happiness and peace for thirty years and maybe we can keep it that way for even longer. However, if you ask Me to perform a miracle, it will be My first one. And when I do, My divinity will become manifest, My divine powers will become known; and when that happens, all those Scribes and Pharisees down in Jerusalem will awaken, which means I will take My first step, and you will come with Me, to the cross." This was the substance of His words.

But Mary sized the thing up beautifully. She simply turned to the caterers without waiting for a positive "yes" from her Son and said, "Do whatever He tells you." At that moment she took upon herself everything that the passion and death of Christ would entail. She understood that before the gates of heaven swung open to her, her Son had to die. Satan in the desert tried to keep Christ away from His cross; Mary at the wedding feast pushed Him toward it. With no concern for herself or for the agony that His death would bring into her own life, but thinking only of the need for the world's redemption, she sent Him on His way to Calvary.

Christ went into action. In the vestibule were six stone urns which were used for ablution. Servants were continually drawing from them to pour water over the hands and feet of the guests, and to dilute the wine which was never taken straight. Christ said, "Fill the jars with water." They obeyed. Then He said, "Draw out now, and take to the chief steward."

About 150 gallons of plain water went into those pots and 150 gallons of fine wine came out. And while He was at it, Christ made the best possible wine. When the servants took the water made into wine to the chief steward, he tasted it, and jokingly said to the groom, "Every man at the beginning doth set forth good wine, and when men have drunk well, then that which is worse. But thou hast kept the good wine until now."

We can imagine how the newlyweds loved Christ for this, for sparing them the tragic and lifelong memory of a wedding feast turned fiasco. He was so gracious about the whole thing. At Cana, Christ made Himself the perfect model of the ordinary life, wishing by His example to sanction a moderate enjoyment of innocent pleasures. By gracing the wedding feast with His presence and a miraculous gift, our Lord took the first step toward raising marriage to the dignity of a sacrament. He had consecrated water to the holy purpose of baptism by His own baptism in the Jordan. Now He pointed to the new dignity that was to be added to the married state which would make a husband and wife, joined under God in the holy sacrament of Matrimony, the very lord and lady of creation itself.

The miracle of changing water into wine was our Lord's first manifestation of His divine power, and it is significant that He worked this miracle at the request of His Blessed Mother. From this day on, the name and the words of Christ would be known to all the world. St. John put it this way: "This first of His signs Jesus worked at Cana of Galilee; and He manifested His glory, and His disciples believed in Him."

Now He had made His move; there was no turning back. It was the beginning of His public career. From now on, He would no longer be the silent Christ wrapped in contemplation of the Father and of the heaven which He left to become a divine D.P. on earth; now He became a name, a figure that would focus the attention of the then known world, the miracle worker in the limelight, the conversation piece at every table. He became the Saviour who would demand of all men, "Are you with Me or against Me?"

The wonder of what He did at Cana would precede Him wherever He went. And down in Jerusalem, the high priest would scan the approaches of the city with eyes like tiny gimlets of misery, waiting for Him to come so that He might be quickly and finally dispatched on the cross of Calvary.

11 ❦ THE TEMPLE PURGE

The wedding feast of Cana had shifted from near death into high life; the miracle of Christ had saved the day. So with the sound of laughter and merriment ringing in His ears, Christ left the party. St. John says: "He went down to Capharnaum, He and His mother, and His brethren, and His disciples. And they stayed there but a few days."

Right here, we should pull up for a moment and get something straight. This word, brethren, for instance! Brethren, as it is used so often in the Scripture, does not mean brothers, as some off-beat segments of society would have it. To say that Christ had blood brothers would be to say that the Blessed Mother was not a virgin; for if Mary had borne other children, then she could not have been a virgin.

And some ingrates would love to deny Mary the beautiful privilege of virginity.

A close study of the Gospel and tradition will prove that the so-called "brethren of the Lord" were, beyond all shadow of doubt, simply His cousins. The word "brother" in the Bible had a much wider meaning than in our language. It was not only used figuratively – as it is used in monastic life when a monk refers to his fellow monks as his brothers – but also in the proper sense to mean near relatives. In Hebrew and Aramaic they just don't have a word for "cousins"; so it was necessary for these people to use the word "brothers" in designating a group of relatives. When we speak of the brethren of Christ, therefore, we do not mean His sisters or His brothers – He had none – but His cousins, which He had.

It was almost time for the feast of the Pasch (a Hebrew word meaning "Passover"). This feast was celebrated in memory of the time in Egypt when the destroying angel killed the first born of the Egyptians, but passed over those Jewish houses that had doorposts sprinkled with the blood of a lamb. So Jesus waited in Capharnaum until the caravan from Galilee went through. He and His Apostles joined the crowd and went on to Jerusalem.

The heart and soul of all Jewish festivities was the Temple. The Temple in existence at the time of Christ had been rebuilt by Herod to proclaim his own glory and to ingratiate him with the Jewish people. The well-known Wailing Wall of modern times is a fragment of Herod's work. He hired 10,000 workers and trained 1000 priests as masons so that they would be able to work on those sacred interiors which the laity were not permitted to enter. The job took forty-six years. The interior court of the Temple was known as the Court of the Priests, closed to everybody else, exclusively and jealously guarded. Outside of this was the Court of the Israelites, for men only. Then came the Court of Women, reserved, obviously, for the Jewish women. Finally, on the outside was the Court of the Gentiles, a giant esplanade, open to all, Jew as well as Gentile.

When Jesus entered the Court of the Gentiles, He blanched at what He saw. It wasn't anything new, He had seen it before on His previous trips; but this time the spectacle before Him really roused His anger. The outer court of the Temple, supposedly a place of prayer, looked more like a South Street market. It was a zoo, echoing and re-echoing with the bellowing of oxen, the bleating of sheep, the cooing of doves, and the hysterical screaming of human beings. For sheer noise, however, the money-changers, brazenly ensconced in portico after portico, carried the day. The whole thing was a horrible spectacle, a real solid-gold mess. A cow in the cathedral vestibule would cause quite a stir. Yet, there in the house of God were the tables of money-changers, piles upon piles of caged doves, stalls filled with oil, incense, and whatever else was needed for various sacrifices, dirty animals, and disrespectful people. No order, no plan; just mass movement, agitation, and turmoil.

Money was behind it all. As Roman subjects, the Jews used Roman coins; but when they came to buy anything for the service of God, their Roman coins had to be changed for sacred money. The wrangling and the squalling that went on over the exchange caused an uproar of such magnitude that one could hardly hear the feeble echo of hymns rising within the inner Temple. Time and again Christ had witnessed this desecration of His Father's house when He had come to worship in the past. This time, things would be different. On this trip He came not only as a worshiper but as an avenger. Now His mission was fully under way, and, in proof of it, He would act directly, openly, as one possessing the authority of God Himself. Not in His own name would He turn this place upside down, but in the name of His Father; and He proceeded to do so.

Taking pieces of cord from around the necks of some oxen, He braided them into a whip; and with arm uplifted and eyes darting fire, He descended in holy rage and righteous anger upon the traders and their merchandise. "My house shall be called the house of prayer for all the nations. But you have made it a den of thieves" (Mk. 11:17). Pandemonium broke loose; it all happened so quickly. Dealers and money-changers took to their heels; terrified beasts stampeded through the tightly packed throngs; people cried out in panic. Moving forward relentlessly, inexorably, Christ upended the money tables, sending silver shekels cascading across the Temple floor, with no one taking time out to scoop them up en route. He didn't even use the scourge; all He did was brandish it. But when He came to the sellers of doves, He was more lenient. Quietly but no less firmly He said, "Take these things away, and do not make the house of My Father a house of business."

Finally He stopped and looked around. The vast enclosure was deserted. There was no order before; there was even less now. Money lay about, waiting to be retrieved by the first brave souls to venture back in. But from above, the priests had been attracted by the fracas. They were the guardians of the Temple who stood to profit financially by the abuses that Christ had just obliterated. So they made their way down and approached Christ, ready to call Him to account for creating such a disturbance. Towering with rage, they were, until they saw the slowly dying fire in His eyes. Then they cooled. Keeping closer together for moral support and putting on a bold front, they asked, "What sign dost Thou show us, seeing that Thou dost these things?"

These men could not say that Christ had done some wrong. They knew the abuse was there; they knew they were sacrilegiously filling their pockets. So they couldn't say, "Why have You done this?" They knew very well why. The best they could say was, "Who do You think You are to take over the job of reformer?" It wasn't an honest question so it didn't deserve an answer. His only reply was, "Destroy this temple, and in three days I will raise it up." He wasn't doing things in a small way now. They asked Him for a sign, maybe just a little one. He gave them the biggest scoop that they would ever hope to hear in a lifetime. He foretold His resurrection from the dead. But they missed it. Earthbound, materialistic, without faith, without understanding, they thought He spoke of the Temple of Herod. They said, "Forty-six years has this temple been in building, and wilt Thou raise it up in three days?"

Christ turned and walked away from them. Later on, when He stood trial, these priests would take these words He had just spoken, twist them, and expedite His execution. They would remember what He said about the destruction and raising of the Temple but they would never understand it. His Apostles would. After His resurrection, His Apostles would remember what He said: "Destroy this temple, and in three days I will raise it up." They would know, when it was all over, what He meant; and it would be such a boon to them and their faith. But now, without explaining, He retraced His steps through the rubble He had caused and went His way.

12 A MIDNIGHT RENDEZVOUS

When Christ took a whip into His hand to silence the jingling of money in the Temple court, He executed an act of authority for which the Jewish leaders never forgave Him. From this moment on, the priests, Pharisees, Sadducees, and Herodians temporarily called a truce to their own little domestic wars and joined their forces in a common hatred for Jesus. Their strategy was one of constant badgering — laying snares to catch Christ in His speech, trying to work up the people against Him, attributing His miracles to the power of Satan, charging Him with breaking the Sabbath and blaspheming against God. All in all, they were a bad lot. All, that is, except one, and his name was Nicodemus.

Nicodemus was a big wheel in the synagogue and a man of great wealth. The Talmud says of him that he could have fed the entire population of Israel for ten days. Clearly he was rich and highly esteemed by his less savory colleagues. But he had obviously been touched by the preaching of John the Baptist. So he wanted to see and speak with Jesus.

Prudence is sometimes a virtue which the comfortably situated highly respect. Nicodemus was an honest man, and upright, too; but his social position evidently required that he be very cautious and prudent about what he did in public. He had the moral sensitivity to recognize truth, but fundamentally he lacked courage. Nicodemus probably believed that Christ was the Messias, but he didn't have the courage to follow Him openly. He didn't have the courage to leave his soft, easy life for the dubious privilege of being with Christ. He was "chicken." Maybe he would follow Christ if it didn't cost too much. At any rate, he would see this Man.

So he went by night. He half believed in our Lord and wanted to be taught by Him, but he was afraid of what people might say. It would never do to have it noised about that a member of the Sanhedrin, a master in Israel, was going for instructions to this new Teacher, the Son of a carpenter. Nicodemus did not want to be the talk of the town so he went to Christ under the cover of darkness, making his way through the deserted streets, and up the outside stairs, stealthily like a cat, ashamed of being caught in the act of visiting God. Then, with the soft light of a candle diffusing their faces, they spent the night in talk.

"Rabbi," said Nicodemus with the respectful tone of a pupil speaking to his teacher, "we know that Thou hast come a teacher from God, for no man can do these signs that Thou workest, unless God be with Him." This was the question in the back of every Jew's mind. Was this really the long-awaited One, the One who would restore the kingdom of God?

Jesus looked right through Nicodemus with a single glance. He was fundamentally a virtuous soul hamstrung by conformity, filled with all kinds of secondhand opinions, but nonetheless deserving of a great new revelation. Shifting Nicodemus' train of thought to a higher level, Christ said, "Amen, amen, I say to thee, unless a man be born again, he cannot see the kingdom of God."

Here, for the first time, Jesus expounds His doctrine. To be born again or to be born from on high (the Greek of the Gospel permits either interpretation) meant to undergo a complete transformation, a transformation that would change men from the level whereon they lived in common with beasts, earthbound, with faces in the dirt, and raise them up to live in common with God, the life of God. What Christ meant in speaking of rebirth to Nicodemus was, "Stop living as beasts. Change. Turn over a new leaf. Begin living as men."

Our friend Nicodemus did not like the sound of all this. He was satisfied with his worldliness. He didn't want to change, not really. So in order to placate his own conscience, he tried to make Jesus' statement seem ridiculous. "How can a man be born when he is old?" he asked. "Can he enter a second time into his mother's womb and be born again?" Christ didn't think there was anything ridiculous about this. He pressed on, more emphatic than ever: "Unless a man be born again of water and the Spirit, he cannot enter into the kingdom of God." Here definitely was the doctrine of Baptism. But Nicodemus looked blank. This poor fellow's trouble was that he lacked any feeling for the things of the spirit. Christ spoke of the wind. The wind cannot be seen, cannot be touched; no one knows where it starts or where it ends, but it is real. Yet the supernatural is far more real than even the wind. It is the spirit that transforms the soul, nothing material. It is the spirit that gives new life to the soul, enabling it to serve God.

Here we are impressed by the obvious fact that Jesus was not just addressing Himself to an honest but fearful man of the Sanhedrin. He was speaking to all men, pouring out His teaching to a waiting world. Nicodemus must have been dreadfully torn in his heart. Wanting to believe, yet afraid to believe. He could not open his mouth now. Christ spoke on in the dim light, passing on to Nicodemus and the world that doctrine that was an advance summary of His whole teaching.

a) God so loved the world that He gave His only-begotten Son – a God made Flesh.

b) Christ came to earth to save mankind, not to condemn it.

c) Like Moses, who saved his people in the desert from the fiery bite of the serpent, so Christ would also bring protection and redemption.

d) Christ would destroy darkness and bring light into the world.

e) Those who followed Christ would have eternal life.

Nicodemus came to Christ in fear, bearing a parched and desolate soul. He came as a worldling, attached to the things of the world. But after his experience, he could never be quite the same man again. He would never forget. He would go back the way he came, in the darkness, unseen and unrecognized; but he would never be able to blot entirely from his mind the new world that Jesus had opened to him. He would remain forever the patron of the millions who would only worship God in secret, but never openly, never with pride. Only in darkness, lest they be discovered on their knees.

Christ didn't change Nicodemus on the spot, but He did win his heart. Later on, at the trial of Jesus, Nicodemus stood up to offer a weak defense, but of course it was no use. Christ was condemned and Nicodemus went to his bed.

The next day the lifeless body of Jesus hung on a cross. His own people had delivered Him up to His death. He had been betrayed by one Apostle, denied by another, forsaken and deserted by all. Mary stood beside His dead body with no one to take Him down from the cross, to give Him a grave, to help bury Him. The Jews were triumphant now. They had tortured Him to death, they had called down His blood upon themselves and their children, they hated His name and all that were His. Then, two men of noble bearing approached the cross. They were the disciples of Jesus, but only in secret. Nobody knew about them. They brought myrrh and aloes and linen cloths. While His Apostles were hiding and His enemies were rejoicing, they reverently took down the sacred body from the cross and bound it in linen cloths with spices, and laid it in a new sepulcher in a garden. And one of them was Nicodemus.

He had never found the courage to follow Christ while the Master was alive. He had never become big enough to leave all, to take up His cross. He had never found the grit to make the first team. But now, with the blood of Christ on his hands and the words of Christ in his ears, Nicodemus must have thrown himself in tears upon the ground and understood it all when a soldier cried out across the hill of Calvary, "Truly, this was the Son of God!"

13 DOWN BY THE WELL

St. Peter didn't think much of the idea, and probably said as much; but when Christ said He was going to take the short cut from Judea to Galilee, He meant it. And the Apostles, liking it or not, followed their Master. Taking the short cut north meant going through the heart of Samaria, something that a good Jew, who valued his skin, just didn't do. The reason, of course, was the idiotic but long-standing feud between the Jews and the Samaritans.

These two factions avoided each other like the plague. Feeling ran so high that a mere glance from one was an insult and cause for battle. There were all sorts of skirmishes. Sometimes, when the Jews lit beacon fires upon the hills to guide the caravans from Galilee to Jerusalem, the Samaritans, devilish scamps that they were, lit false beacon fires which had the Jews milling around in circles at night, lost, and wondering who had moved Jerusalem. Things got so bad that the Jews avoided Samaria completely, even though it meant going down the east bank of the Jordan and crossing the river twice.

Generations before, Samaritans had fraternized and intermarried with Gentile invaders. This made them half-breeds, so to speak; half Gentile and half Jewish. Because of such defilement of Jewish blood, the Jews refused to let the Samaritans help in the construction of the Temple. So the Samaritans got their backs up, built their own temple, worshiped their own idols – and the fight was on.

It was small wonder, then, that the Apostles felt misgivings about the trip across Samaria, looking back over their shoulders as they went, fearing what might lurk behind every rock and every bush. They felt quite miserable about the whole journey, while Jesus, serene and secretly smiling at their groundless discomfort, led them on. At high noon they drew near the town of Sichem. After about five hours of toil on the dusty road, Jesus was tired. His divinity did not save Him from weariness and fatigue. He was like us in every way except sin. And right now He wanted to stop for a rest.

By the side of the road was a very old well that had been dug by Jacob and given by him to his son Joseph. It was highly prized by the people, not only for its historical and sentimental value, but also for its depth and abundance of fresh water – a rarity in the area. The plan of Jesus required that He be alone, so He told His Apostles to hop on into Sichem to get something to eat. They didn't know what to get from the Samaritans, but they had their orders and went to fulfill them. Jesus sat by the side of the well, the Hunter baiting His trap, the Shepherd seeking the sheep. He waited.

The stage was set, and in a short while the woman advanced toward the well. She was a buxom, vital, peasant girl, a solid-gold beauty, the *femme fatale* of Sichem; and she came alone to the well at noon because she was entirely ostracized by the other women who came for water like a twittering horde in the evening. She wore a green hood thrown back from her head and she had a jug slung over her shoulder. The sight of a Jew sitting at the well surprised her, but, being a patriotic sort of Samaritan, intent on keeping the old feud in a state of agitation, she decided to snub Him. She busied herself with tying ropes to the handles of her jug and lowering it into the darkness of the well. She was not the type of girl who shocked easily, but she was shocked now at the very simple fact that this Jew spoke to her.

He said, "Give Me to drink." We don't know whether she gave Him a drink or not. Probably not. Probably she didn't even hear what He said. It was surprise enough that He spoke. What she wanted to know, and she said it, was what business did this Jew have speaking to her, a Samaritan. Jesus gave her an answer, "If thou didst know . . . who it is who says to thee: 'Give Me to drink,' thou, perhaps, wouldst have asked of Him, and He would have given thee living water."

Maybe she thought this was ridiculous enough to laugh at, maybe she was honestly puzzled; but at least she was practical. She tried to illustrate the foolishness of what He said by pointing out that He did not have a ladle or a pitcher or anything with which to get the water from the well. So how could He give her a drink? Then Christ hit her with this: "Who drinks of this water will thirst again. He, however, who drinks of the water that I will give him shall never thirst." She was overwhelmed. She answered Him, "Give me this water that I may not thirst."

Jesus had secured what He wanted, her faith. It was not much, but it was a beginning. Now He would do what He had done to Peter and Nathanael, read her heart and her mind. He would let her see that nothing was hidden from Him. "Go, call thy husband." The command flustered her. With a toss of her pretty head she answered, "I have no husband" (for she did value this Stranger's good opinion of her). Christ spoke and His voice was so low she could scarcely hear Him, "Thou hast said well, 'I have no husband,' for thou hast had five husbands, and he whom thou now hast is not thy husband. In this thou hast spoken truly." If anyone else had said it, it would have been a stinging taunt, its very truth driving her away in shame; but coming from Him it was different. In some ways she was glad He knew. Now, womanlike, she would see this through, turn the conversation from herself to Him, change the subject. As if to placate a dangerous man, she reminded Him that He should be merciful to her because their common ancestors worshiped on this mountain. Her face was growing paler, her body trembling. It was a relief, when, after a long pause, He spoke to her, "Woman . . . God is a spirit, and they who worship Him must worship in spirit and in truth."

This was a statement that tore away all grounds for battle between Jerusalem and Samaria; but it was too vast a truth to reach her, whose heart was too often broken, too often dragged through the mud. She said only what she knew: "I know that the Messias is coming (who is called Christ), and when He comes He will tell us all things." This was her confession of faith. She had already called Him a Prophet; now she declared her belief in a Messias and her readiness to accept Him when He came. Jesus had waited for this moment. He had led her on from a cup of water to the promise of living water; from death to confession and revival; from a blinding vision of light to an act of faith in the Messias if she ever came to know Him.

This was farther than He had reached with anyone; He would reward her in a unique way. To this sinful woman, He would make the first public announcement of His messianic mission: "I who speak with thee am He." The hungry heart of Christ craving to be known! He would not make another statement like this until He stood before His judges. But now, because He loved all creatures, saints and sinners, He came down into this woman's own gutter to tell her He was the Son of God.

The return of the Apostles just then put her to flight. She ran, the scarlet woman, the lost sheep, the immoral nobody, she ran screaming through the streets of Sichem, announcing the arrival of the Messias in their midst. Ordinarily, the people who came running to their front doors would not have put much faith in what this particular girl had to say; but now they believed her. They had to. They followed her, the Pied Piper of the Lord, back to the well. Out there they found the Apostles trying to get their Master to eat, and Him saying, "My food is to do the will of Him who sent Me"; for while others longed for the food of the body, He longed to do His Father's will that men might be redeemed. . . . The Samaritans took Him into their midst where He remained for two days.

Later on, when the Jews had rejected Him, He would think of these happy days at Sichem, and whenever He wanted to teach a lesson of gratitude or kindness to strangers, He used as His example the Samaritans. At that moment when He watched this woman spreading the news of

His arrival, He must have thought of the day to come, one of the brightest in history, when another woman, just like this one, would hasten from an empty tomb to tell the world, "I have seen the Lord."

The remarkable thing about both these girls who proclaimed the good news through the streets of the world — both of them were sinners.

14 FULL OF LEPROSY

We are hands and feet, we are eyes and ears, we are creatures of our senses; that is why we can easily believe what we see, and feel, and smell. But today Christ is not visible as He was in those wonderful days when He walked our earth; and although He is just as real now as He was then, there are passing moments in our lives when we wish we could see Him, "just to be sure." Our faith takes a nose dive and we stand, unarmed and trembling, before the hot blasts of unbelief. At a time like this, we should pick up our New Testament and read through this particular phase of Christ's life. For these were the days of great and numerous miracles, when He called forth His divine powers to perform miracles of such wonderment that He left people bug-eyed from what they had seen.

On the face of it, Christ was an extraordinary man, a foreteller of the future, a wonder-worker, but above all He was a healer of souls. If He had been concerned only about men's bodies, He could have made bread grow on trees (so we would never be hungry) or money fall from the sky (so we would never be poor). But if He did this He would have deprived us of the one thing that makes us super creatures – suffering.

Christ performed miracles to give poor creatures release from their suffering, only to see them run away from Him, for a world that is always prosperous and joyous easily forgets Christ. Christ did not perform miracles just to straighten limbs, to put sight into eyes, or to keep men's stomachs filled. Christ performed miracles to prove His divinity, to strengthen people's faith, and to express His divine compassion and love of humans. Thousands of pilgrims journey to Lourdes, looking only for outward healing and forgetting that inward healing – conversion or renewed faith in God – is the real purpose of the miracles.

But these were days of miracles. The whole country was talking about Him. Women picking lentils in the fields praised His kindness. Hucksters sitting in the market place, dark-skinned traders stacking their bolts of silk and baskets of linen, day laborers waiting to be hired – all sorts of men admired and trusted Him. Homemakers at their ovens, millers throwing chaff and grain against the morning breeze with their winnowing shovels, farmers in their fields praying for deliverance from the locusts, trappers in the hills seeking partridge and deer and perhaps a bear that strayed down from Mount Hermon – all the city at its daily work talked about Jesus.

But things were not going too well in Peter's house. He had been tagging after John the Baptist for quite a spell; now he was following Jesus, and his fish business was suffering. He had always been an honest, hard-working man, but now he was a dreamy sort of person with his nets dry and his boat badly in need of a calking job. Naturally this must have upset Peter's home. It may even have caused friction. Both his wife and his wife's mother who lived with them must have wondered about the strange spell which the Stranger from Nazareth had cast over Peter, over them all. Peter might have developed "mother-in-law trouble," for all we know – and just then his mother-in-law fell ill.

Nothing to trifle with was her illness, no mere headache or any other of the million ailments that some women like to enjoy. There was glaze over her eye, dryness in the throat, flushed cheeks, and burning forehead – the fever prevalent in the low country after the first rains of autumn. And it was deadly. When Peter returned and saw her condition, he immediately sent for the physician, who arrived likely with his little black bag. With stethoscope, medicine, pills? Not at all! He brought his ashes from a charred wolf's skull, heads of mice, eyes of crabs, owls' brains, salt of vipers' sweat, frogs' livers, and elephant lice – the works! Nothing helped. Naturally. So Peter got smart and went after Jesus.

Jesus came in, walked to the sickbed, touched the woman's hand. She turned away from Him, hostile at first because she may have felt that here was the Man who had disrupted the even tenor of their lives. But then she turned back with a bewildered air, not knowing how to account for the instant change that swept over her. She had been dying; now she was well. She jumped out of bed, prepared supper for Jesus and His followers, and from that moment on was the best little mother-in-law that anyone ever had.

By sunset the whole town had heard about it and came storming Peter's door, filling the yard and choking the street. They hobbled on crutches; they crawled on their knees. The strong carried the weak. The insane came for mental release. There were people with pain and fevers, boils and cancers; the crippled, the hunchbacked, the blind, and the dumb. And upon them all Jesus laid His firm, cool hands. He bought down the mercy of His Father until the hunchbacks stood straight, the mute spoke, the blind beheld for the first time the beautiful, perspiring face of Christ – all of them crying out, "You are indeed the Son of God."

The miracles continued. Later on, down at the lake, Christ told His Apostles to let down their nets. Peter was sympathetic, shaking his head at the naïve Carpenter who knew nothing about fishing. But to honor Him, Peter let down his net where he knew there were no fish. And his catch almost broke his net.

Then, having left the lake, they were trudging along the road when a miserable object that had escaped detection darted from its hiding place and threw itself in His path. It was a man, or a semblance of one, anyway; a figure in such frightful and repulsive state that he appeared scarcely human. Coarse, white hair hung down over what was to have passed for a face – eyes glassy and staring, eyelids and lips gone, cheeks eaten away by disease, neck and hands covered with white scales. Luke, the physician, diagnosed the case right on the spot with brevity and certainty: He was "full of leprosy."

This wretch was a living dead man, an outcast of society, banished from home and friends and forced to live like an animal in a cave. He had no business in the city because he was forbidden to approach his fellow men. He carried with him the corruption of the grave, he polluted the air around him. Without shelter or food or medicine he wandered about, an object of fear and horror to all. If people came near him, he was bound to cry out, "Unclean!" Men shouted and threw rocks at him, reviled him, not because he was wicked, but because he was a leper.

This poor leper knew he was breaking the law, but he had heard that Jesus healed every deformity. So he lay at the feet of Christ, hiding his disfigured face in the dirt, praying, "Lord, if Thou wilt, Thou canst make me clean." No demands, no threats, but complete faith, as if he said, "If God wills it, heal me; if not, then I am resigned." The words of Christ came back as an echo of his own, "I will. Be thou made clean." A word would have been enough to effect a cure, but Christ bent down and touched him. He was not afraid. He was not going to shrink from a loathsome disease, because, in view of what He knew about the ugliness of sin, leprosy was beautiful.

Today, much of the world is leprous with sin. Nor could any leprous body be nearly so hideous as a soul in the state of mortal sin. Which is worse? Leprosy can destroy only a body; mortal sin can destroy a soul. And a lost soul is the most horrible, most irreparable thing that could ever be imagined.

We needn't worry about leprosy of the body. It is so rare in our country. But we do have to worry about leprosy of the soul, a condition not nearly so rare. Whether we have one or the other, we can always be certain of this: if we carry our afflictions to Christ and throw ourselves in humble prayer at His feet, crying, "Lord, if Thou wilt, Thou canst make me clean," we can be sure of His answer: "I will. Be thou made clean."

15 DOUBLE MIRACLE

Fan clubs, we are told, are an American institution. Smart public-relations men, whose job it is to build popularity for celebrities of the entertainment world, thought up the fan club as the easiest way out. Stars of stage and screen are strongly in favor of fan clubs, for it is the nationally organized fan club that keeps their pockets well filled with greenbacks. And American teen-agers, not all but too many of them, go all out for these rackets while the public-relations men stand in the wings, smiling at their gullibility.

Christ, the God-Man, in His public life stands out in historically sharp contrast. Christ needed no public-relations agency to further His popularity with the common people. He, alone, was enough. He alone, in His love, had appeal so great, so universally great, that His Apostles frequently tried to keep the people away, that He might get a little rest. Christ's popularity did not need the artificial stimulation of public-relations gimmicks. Yet no one in the history of the world had so many, such loving, such devoted, such grateful followers as Christ had. His very presence brought such vast crowds, caused such unrestrained demonstrations, that at times He found Himself retiring to the country. Now He seldom entered a town openly, but would remain outside in the desert, praying. These were days of much prayer for Him.

Later, when much of the excitement had abated, He would return to His favorite town, Capharnaum. But at this time, His popularity with the common people had made Him very unpopular with the ruling set from Jerusalem. He had been making all of them look silly and they didn't like it. So the spies were out, following Him, with orders from headquarters to "get something on Him." And He was going to oblige them. He was going to give them a real scoop to take back to the Holy City.

One day a vast crowd of "first nighters" had gathered around a house in Capharnaum. Christ was inside. Everybody was there, even the Pharisees and the doctors of the law from every town of Galilee and Judea and from Jerusalem. The mob in the street had no way of getting inside the house; it was bursting at the seams. The best they could expect was a glimpse of Him when He came out. They would have to wait.

But on the outer fringe of the crowd there were five men who could not wait. Four of them were toting a mattress, the fifth was on it — a paralytic without the use of his speech or his limbs, strapped by horrible internal suffering, and shaking uncontrollably. They couldn't muscle their way through such a mob, so they came up with an idea. The house was like all the others, one story with a flat roof. These men moved their piteous burden around to the side of the house, up the steps, and onto the roof. There they found what they expected to find, an opening covered with slates.

No one inside the house knew it, but they were about to be disturbed. The foursome on the roof removed the slates that covered the opening. With much noise, of course, they incurred the consummate displeasure of those within the house. A hole large enough to admit the mattress was made and the paralyzed man was lowered by ropes into the midst of the crowd and set to rest at the feet of Christ.

The Master interrupted His speaking to watch the whole operation with some amusement. The paralytic lay helpless on the floor; his four friends looked down through the hole in the roof, their eyes reflecting the sureness and the faith within them. Here Christ made an astonishing move. He did not tell the cripple to arise and walk. Instead, He said to the hopeless case at His feet, "Man, thy sins are forgiven thee."

No sooner were these words spoken than the enemies of Christ stiffened in shocked surprise. They had been expecting a miracle, more or less; they never counted on a statement of such bold exactitude. They thought within themselves, "Who is this man who speaks blasphemies? Who can forgive sins, but God only?" And how right they were! Who, indeed, but God could forgive sins! It could have been a revelation to them; it could have borne witness to the fact that if this Jesus could forgive sins, then He was truly the Son of God. But their minds did not work that way. It was too pat, too logical; and their big mistake was in thinking that Jesus was merely a man.

The Saviour read their minds. "Why are you arguing in your hearts? Which is easier, to say, 'Thy sins are forgiven thee,' or to say, 'Arise and walk'? But that you may know that the Son of Man has power on earth to forgive sins" – He said to the man sick of palsy – "I say to thee, arise, take up thy pallet and go to thy house."

To cure an incurable disease and to forgive sins are equally easy to talk about and equally hard to do. They presuppose infinite power. If Christ had the power to do one, He had the power to do the other. But He wanted to show these people something. He couldn't very well prove the visible miracle (curing a paralytic) by resorting to an invisible miracle (forgiving a sinner); but He could do the opposite and He did. When the man on the mat sat up, got to his feet, picked up his bed, and started through the crowd glorifying God as he went, this was proof enough that Christ could destroy sin with a word.

It makes us very happy to know that Christ could forgive the sins of this poor man. But what about us? Christ ascended into heaven centuries ago. Who will forgive our sins? Or was forgiveness given only to those lucky few who lived in His time? The simple answer comes as a relief. What a man possesses and owns, he can give away. And He did. To Peter when He said, "Whose sins you shall forgive, they are forgiven," and to every other successor of the Apostles, the priests whom you see every day. They have the power given to them by Christ through Peter and his successors.

We are lucky people. When we go to confession, we know our sins are forgiven. Getting on our knees and telling almighty God that we are sorry for having sinned might seem more convenient, but not quite so satisfying. Besides, to pass up confession is to pass up a good deal. Priests,

Brothers, and Sisters go into that box once a week, not because they are the world's greatest sinners (there are greater), but because they realize what confession is. They know that the confessional is not just a place to dump their sins (it's that, of course, and good riddance to them), but a place wherein God awaits their coming so that He might flood their souls and enrich their lives with the gift of His grace. And grace isn't just a girl's name. It is strength to overcome evil desires. It is courage to keep going in the face of repeated failures. It is wisdom to make us see that the life Christ led is the only kind of life to lead.

Furthermore, that paralytic wasn't afraid to have his sins forgiven. Some people are. Some teen-agers go to confession with the idiotic notion that the priest (who's quite shockproof) will be shocked at their sins. But no teen-ager can tell a priest-confessor anything he hasn't heard before.

A good confession requires sorrow for our sins, a firm desire to avoid in the future anything that might cause us to sin again, and, above all, honesty. As for the fellow or girl who is not honest in the box, who through fear or shame refuses to make a good confession, choosing instead the hard remorseful road of sacrilege – that poor person is in a bad way. For the hand of the priest, which would have been raised to bring down the pardon of sin, might bring down upon the dishonest penitent a reserved seat on the brink of hell itself.

We had better not forget the story of the paralytic who got more than he had asked for. It was the first time men had ever heard from human lips the assurance of God's forgiveness of sin. "Thy sins are forgiven thee." It was no wonder that the crowds went away, saying in hushed tones, "We have seen wonderful things today." And they weren't talking about the physical angle of the miracle. They had seen that kind before. They had witnessed something for which mankind had been hungry through long centuries – a positive assurance that they could be released from the crushing burden of sin. It was this positive assurance that prompted the famous convert, Gilbert K. Chesterton, to say, "The only reason I became a Catholic was to make sure my sins would be forgiven."

16 RECIPE FOR HAPPINESS

When Christ openly and publicly forgave the sins of the paralytic, He pushed the button that started the wheels of a great conspiracy turning – wheels that would never stop until He was securely fastened to His cross. But before this happened, He had two things to do, two very important things.

First of all, He had to complete the selection of His followers so that they would be able to carry on after He was gone. Back in Capharnaum, He sent out Peter and James to bring ten others, whom He named, from among the throng that helpfully followed Him wherever He went. An hour later twelve men stood in a circle around Him on an isolated part of the pebbly shore of the lake.

Impulsive, weather-tanned Peter with his freckled nose was there, of course, and his tall brother, Andrew. Then there was Bartholomew, also called Nathanael; the bright-eyed, impetuous John; his brother, James the Greater; the exuberant, ex-tax collector, Matthew; and the muscular, athletic Philip – all of these were relatively old-timers in His service.

The new ones included James the Less, who, nearly forty years later, was for the love of Christ to be thrown from the top of the Temple, and being seen still to breathe, finally stoned to death. Standing next to him was his young brother, Jude, who, in sixty years from this June afternoon, was to be murdered by Armenian arrows. Still another brother, Simon, would one day be nailed to an X-like cross in Persia. Also in the group stood Thomas, the Doubter, who, on some later day, doubting no longer, was to be ripped with a spear in India. Finally, there was Judas Iscariot of whom nothing more need be said.

This hybrid crew of twelve, chosen from all walks of life, received their orders. With the recent death of John the Baptist, it was important that their mission begin at once. They must do and teach as Christ had been doing; they must cure, heal, and relieve the oppressed in the manner of Christ. He had taken His first step in the final preparation; now He must take His second step. He led them – the crowds again falling into line – up beside the lake. There, having settled down, He sealed His death warrant by His Sermon on the Mount.

This sermon included the oft-mentioned Eight Beatitudes, a series of rules to keep a man serene and capable in the midst of any disaster. It contained the highest ideals ever offered to men. Never until that moment, and never since, has the world heard so concise, so orderly a statement of how we can live a full happy life on earth. None of this "how to win friends" nonsense, nor "how to live 365 days a year." None of "how to kid yourself along by avoiding all the hard things in life." This was the recipe for the making of a real man. Here was all that ever need be known about God, creation, and daily life; here, too, were the most audacious promises ever made to humanity. And the interesting thing about it all was that Christ did not play the huckster, selling His wares. He did not promise them pie in the sky, cigarette trees, or foam-rubber cushions. He offered no guarantee against pain, loss, grief, or disgrace. He did not promise them, then or ever, material comforts for their devoted service. His promises were of things eternal. In brief, "Do this on earth and I will reward you with this in Heaven."

His eight rules, called Beatitudes (which means that they bring happiness), were simple and wise, but difficult to follow. The way to destruction was broad as a river; the way to glory was straight and narrow. To follow them was a surefire answer to man's quest for happiness both here and in eternity; to reject them for the rules of the world was to end up in a heap of ashes at the end of the road.

His teaching here beat to death a hoard of modern concepts. He never said, "Blessed are the Joneses with TV's in every room, two cars in the garage, and a recreation room in the basement, for they will keep ahead of everybody." He did not say, "Blessed is the high school girl who wears Persian Melon Lipstick (which drives men mad in daylight and insane at night), for she shall be called 'cool kitty from Kansas City.'" Nor did He say, "Blessed is the high school boy who spends his evenings in a parked car with his 'steady,' for he shall never bear the title, 'square bear from nowhere.'" For these are the pagan, animal beatitudes that bring everything *but* true happiness.

"Blessed are the poor in spirit" meant that a man should not bend all his efforts for the accumulation of wealth alone. It required him to be gentle, humble; not heady, proud, or arrogant. If he succeeds in one task, he is not to sit back and gloat and drag, but go right on planning another job, a harder one, a better one. It was not a condemnation of money as such; it was a warning to have at all times a deep sense of our nothingness (poverty) before God and our need for Him.

"Blessed are the meek" was not meant to make a Christian a cringing coward; it was just a blow at jealousy and envy. It was aimed at making a man at all times patiently resigned to the will of God.

"Blessed are they who mourn" did not tend to make snivelers out of us, or pessimists, or professional weepers. It was, first of all, "Be sorry for your sins." Then develop a deep, glowing sense of compassion for the sufferings of the world, so that men of all nations who weep will have your shoulders to cry on.

"Blessed are they who hunger and thirst for justice" referred to those who so yearned for holiness, which is complete abandonment to the will of God, that they would rather die than ever commit a deliberate sin. The hunger and thirst here is not physical. Christ was not in favor of starvation; He fed too many people on too many hillsides to be accused of encouraging starvation.

"Blessed are the merciful" was a condemnation of selfishness which is something proper to hell and its inhabitants. As we show mercy, so we receive it. We get what we give. Forgive and pardon and we enrich our lives. Hate and seek revenge, and we get it all right back, and more than we ever counted on.

"Blessed are the pure of heart" was a cry for virtue and a control of lust, not as a denial of love but as a guarding of it until the body can be used as God intended it. A youth caught in the slavery of impurity will not see straight, he will not see the harm he does to himself or to the Mystical Body of Christ. Above all, he will not see God.

"Blessed are the peacemakers" was a condemnation of politicians who start wars for the furthering of their own ambitions; and of industrialists who encourage wars for the filling of their own pockets.

"Blessed are they who suffer persecution" was a plea

for followers of such courage and conviction that even the threat and the fact of death would never cause them to betray Christ.

With His Sermon on the Mount, Christ changed the world, then and now. The modern "beatitudes" concerning security, revenge, indifference, cruelty, popularity, sex, armed might, and betrayal, do not belong in the world.

We must make our choice, God's beatitudes or the world's.

17 ❦ THE WORLD'S GREATEST PRAYER

Jesus Christ, in the Sermon on the Mount, really changed the world. With an eternally indelible pen, He put a big period at the end of the Old Testament, for it was finished. And He ushered in a whole new era with the New Testament. It was not Christ's intention to wipe out the Old Testament and the Ten Commandments which are in it. Nor did He. He merely put a finishing stroke to that epoch – for the time covered by the Old Testament was a period of justice, which too often meant an eye-for-an-eye. And He brought with Him an entirely new concept of living – His own era of love. As God, Christ would not abolish justice, for there must always be justice. What He did, rather, was to temper justice with charity, with love. Christ, in effect, said to justice, "Move over and make room for Me. I am Love."

Nor was this sermon a complete synopsis of all His teaching. It was only the fundamental spirit upon which all His other teachings would be built. Notice that He failed to mention many other basic things; He left other points of supreme importance untouched and unhinted. For instance, He made no mention of Baptism in His Sermon, He made no mention of the Eucharist, or of the Church, or of the end of the world; and without these we can never find a true, full picture of His teachings. The Sermon on the Mount gave us the Golden Rule, but there is much more to the following of Christ than simply "doing unto others what you would have them do unto you." For the time being, though, Christ said all that He thought needed saying. The rest would come later. When they were ready for it. But not yet.

What put the crowning glory on this famous sermon to the truth-starved people of Israel was His gift of the Lord's Prayer. Oh, He had been teaching His Apostles about prayer. He set them an example by praying Himself. He made sure that they saw Him slipping off now and then to make private communion with His heavenly Father. He tried repeatedly to impress upon them their absolute inability to do anything at all useful without the help of God. And the only possible way open to those who would reach out for God was prayer.

In other words, Christ wanted to put His followers on the inner track to another and a better life, the spiritual life. Looking about at these people, some of whom had no more spiritual life than the family cat, He tried to establish one for them. There was more to existence than what met the eye. The world about them, the world that they could see, was but a johnny-come-lately thing, only a few billion years old, give or take a year. But eternity, the beginning and the end of all life, the real life, was in fact something entirely spiritual. He tried to create in them an awareness of the supernatural, but they who were but men of the soil and men of the sea were hard put, indeed, to grasp such notions. He told them about prayer. He showed them by His own practices. Still they were foggy about it. So it was as if He took them patiently by the hand, sat them down beside Him, and said, "Do not try to reach God with loud noises as if He were deaf. When you pray, pray like this. Try this method." Then He gave to them and to the world His *Pater Noster*.

"Our Father, who art in heaven." No longer is God only the Master, King, the terrible mighty Jehovah, the Lord of battle before whom all the world trembles. He is our Father. We are His children, all of us – white, black, red, or green. But if we don't accept the brotherhood of man, then we had better skip this prayer altogether.

"Hallowed be Thy name, Thy kingdom come, Thy will be done on earth as it is in heaven." Later on in this prayer we are going to ask God for gifts; but first we want to win God's favor. So with these statements, we let God know we want to be with Him. We want His name to be a name respected in our midst, never permitting it to be used lightly or tossed into the gutter. In other words, we are telling Him that we are going to clean out our own mouths and use His holy name only in a reverent manner. Next, we want Him to know that we are playing on His team in the battle between heaven and hell. We want His kingdom to rule over all kingdoms, those of men and those of Satan. "Thy will be done on earth as it is in heaven" is another way of saying, "God, You don't have any trouble with the people in heaven, but You do have trouble with us. So down here, no matter what happens to me, no matter how many sufferings come into my life, no matter how little I have, it is okay with me because You know what You are doing. You want it this way. So I will find You down here not only in the things that are beautiful and sweet, but I will see Your loving hand in the difficult and the tragic."

With our friendship for God well sealed, we start begging.

"Give us this day our daily bread." We don't want the moon. We just want enough to get along on, just enough to make our lives decent and happy. We don't want a million dollars; just enough wealth to bear our share of the load, and to satisfy within reason our material needs. But, so much more than that, we want the "supersubstantial bread" – we want Christ in Holy Communion.

"Forgive us our trespasses as we forgive those who trespass against us." This is like saying: "Look, God, I forgive my enemies, all of them. I'm forgiving them so that You will let Your forgiveness fall upon me." But here again, if we are not going to forgive our enemies, we had better not utter a word when the Our Father is said. We had better pull that zipper shut right across our mouth. We're just making a joke, a farce, out of it. And we don't make jokes with God.

"Lead us not into temptation but deliver us from evil." Lord, it is rough down here. At times it is so hard to be good. It hardly seems worth the trouble. This is where we need You. So please come with the help, so that we might always be bigger than the temptations around us, Amen.

This is the Our Father, the prayer we all know. And if we could keep only one page from the Gospels, and lose all the rest, this is the page to keep.

The Our Father is short and to the point. It wastes no words. It is simple and direct. It says everything that needs saying. It is the very prayer that Christ Himself taught us from His own lips. And if we say it often enough, and well enough, we might get a peek into the real life, the spiritual life, and come to understand that the house we live in and the car we drive will some day turn to dust, but the God of love and the God we follow will go on for ever and ever. And we will stand beside Him.

18 THE CONQUEST OF DEATH

The sermon on the Mount was over. The people were stunned. The Son of God had changed their entire outlook on life. The "dog-eat-dog" theory was scrubbed right out. The "survival-of-the-fittest" philosophy was dumped right back into the animal kingdom where it belonged. Now the only thing left in life was love. Maybe after the magic spell of His words had left them and they had given a very practical consideration to what He had said, maybe then they were skeptical about it. This was some life, a great one to talk about, to wish for, to dream of — but to live it? That was something else again.

The Saviour understood how they felt. He always understood. As if to place the stamp of authority on what He said, to confirm their faith, to prove that He was speaking as God, then He would show them. He would act as God. So off He went, with the not-quite-convinced crowd at His heels. The greatest drama of all time was on the road!

The first remarkable event took place just on the outskirts of Capharnaum at a place called Bethania, where a small contingent of Roman troops was billeted. Standing at the side of the road, waiting for the approaching Christ, was a Roman officer, a centurion. In the American army he would have been a first lieutenant, possibly a captain. Ordinarily, Jews did not care a hill of beans for Roman soldiers, but this particular soldier was different. He had always shown extreme courtesy and understanding toward the subjugated Jewish nation. He had assisted the townspeople in many small ways; he had even helped them build their temple, an act of kindness which no Jew could ever forget.

Working with the Jews as he did, sharing their gossip, he had heard much about the Great Jew, Jesus. Now he needed Him. His servant, his young Jewish valet, was dying – and nobody could do anything about it. So he stopped Christ on the dusty road and poured out his sad story. Christ offered to come immediately to cure his servant, but from the mouth of this unbeliever came the great prayer of belief, a prayer that has been etched forever in the minds of men, a prayer that finds unique presence in the Sacrifice of the Mass, "Lord, I am not worthy that Thou shouldst enter under my roof . . . only say the word."

By this time Jesus should have been used to anything. But the faith of this Roman pagan so amazed Him that He proclaimed to all around Him, "Not even in Israel have I found so great a faith." It was, on one hand, a gentle condemnation of His own people who had rejected Him so often, in so many ways; it was, on the other hand, a revelation of the fact that He came, not only to the Jews, but to all men. The Jews had no monopoly on Him, so they had better look to their laurels. Christ then cured the centurion's servant without even going into his house. He merely said the word – and it was done! Christ loved faith. He must have grown tired of proving things to the Jews. What He wanted was their trust when it was hard to trust, their faith when it was hard to believe. For faith is the measure of love and the proof of it.

Then, from Bethania He went south with His followers. They covered about twenty-five miles and arrived toward evening at the town of Naim. Naim is a Hebrew word meaning "beautiful." Maybe it was a beautiful town in those days, but today it is a shabby little place, filled with about two hundred Moslems. However, at the gate of the town two crowds converged; Christ and His friends going in, and a funeral procession coming out.

This funeral was like all of them – dreary, sad affairs, exuding through the air that sense of loss and separation which oppresses even the unconcerned. But there was a double tragedy involved here. The corpse, stiff in death and covered with a shroud was that of a very young man who had barely tasted the deep joy of living – this was the first tragedy. The second tragedy was the mother, who happened to be a widow, with nobody else in the world, no husband, no children, nobody. The whole town followed the procession, doing the only thing they could, hoping by their presence to share the grief of this mother. Even the hired mourners, whose profession it was to scream and lament at funerals, must have felt some really honest pangs of sorrow.

With everybody in the village so affected, how could Christ, the Great Consoler, be untouched by what He saw here? The difference between Him and the crowd was that the crowd could do absolutely nothing about it. He could. And He did. He stepped out into the path of the procession, raised His hand, and halted the cortege. It was bad manners to stop a funeral; it was scandalous, in fact. But Christ was not concerned here with silly customs. He had action in mind. So with everybody staring at the interruption, and wondering, He walked over to the sorrowing mother and His great Heart went out to her. Because she was suffering, so was He.

Softly and gently, so as not to jar her, He said, "Do not weep." Bent as she was under the weight of her grief, and blinded by her tears, she could not see Him. She only heard the words, "Do not weep." Words – that was all she had been hearing since her son died. People coming in, telling her to get some rest, telling her that time would heal the wound – the same old, empty mouthings, because there was nothing else that they could say or do. Nothing will bring my boy back, the mother moaned.

Nothing will bring him back, you say, little woman? My, how wrong you are. Wipe away your tears and raise your head so that you will see who it is, telling you not to weep. Then watch Him move with complete assurance to the body of your son. And listen as, in a clear voice, He reaches down into the black pit of death, "Young man, I say to thee, arise."

Immediately, a tremor ran through the shroud. The corpse began to move. It sat up. The arms went up and snatched the cloth from its face. The eyes opened and looked straight into the eyes of Christ. The boy rose to his feet, healthy and well. Alive! Then followed the touching little ceremony when Christ took him by the arm, led him for a few steps, then placed his now warm hand into the cold hand of his mother. Formally, He gave them to each other. And He was happy in their joy.

The impossible fact, of course, dawned slowly in the minds of the crowd. They could not believe what they had seen. It was impossible. But gradually, the truth of it, the real, factual, eyewitness truth broke upon them and they swarmed about Christ crying, "A great prophet has risen among us," and "God hath visited His people." The result of the whole incident was this: His friends were strengthened in friendship, but His enemies were confirmed in their hatred.

Jesus rarely talked about death. He mentioned it a few times. Death was no problem to Him here; its conquest was a snap. He raised this young man to life with about as much effort as it would take Him to blink His eye. And this is our consolation. We must die, certainly. Our hands which today are soft and pink and flexible will, on some tomorrow, be white and cold with a rosary wrapped around them, while we go off to the cemetery in the nicest Cadillac we ever rode in. But we need never fear it. For we will no sooner close our eyes in death than we will hear the voice of Christ calling to us from the vaulted vistas of eternity, "I say to thee, arise."

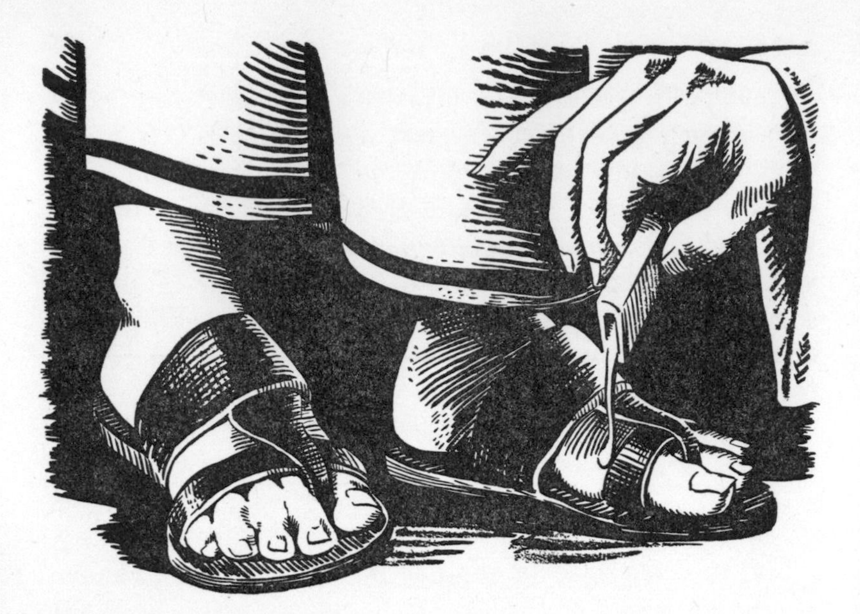

19 ❦ THE WOMAN WHO WENT STRAIGHT

In Naim, Christ gave the gift of life to a body; now in Magdala, He would give life to a soul. Magdala, on the north shore of the Lake of Galilee, was a resort town, and a real "snooty" one at that. It was the Riviera of Palestine, dotted with beautiful, sprawling villas of wealthy Gentiles and Jews. It was a gay town, pandering to the rich and the sensual. But to the ordinary people living in the general area it was strictly "off limits" – a dyed-in-the-wool city of sin.

The proudest boast of Magdala was that it was broad-minded, which is just another way of saying that it was peppered with indifferentism. The bored, fat citizens did not believe in any religion, but got a kick out of them all.

Religion was laughs for them. So when it was learned that Jesus was coming through town on His way north, a few of the city fathers put their thick heads together and decided to stage a party for this interesting Person. It should be a real lark. They could meet Jesus on their own ground, make Him feel a bit ridiculous, show Him that the town was not afraid of anybody, and possibly turn up some of His weak points. All their friends would get a real "charge" out of it.

The lot of being host fell to Simon, a banker of much means and a Pharisee, more tolerant than the rest of his plush-bottom crowd. Personally, though, he was very interested in this Man of whom the whole country was speaking, especially after that business down in Naim. Simon had known John the Baptist who was the sensation the season before; but John seemed something of a fanatic, eating only the produce of the desert. Jesus, on the other hand, was known to be favorable toward a good dinner and did not seem to mind the company He kept at table. Altogether, Simon thought, this Man would be worth meeting; and to have Him for dinner would be an interesting experience he could share with his friends. So the invitation went out and Simon had no idea what a devastating evening he was scheduling for himself.

The invitation was accepted, and when Jesus arrived at Simon's house He realized that they were out to ridicule Him – as if He hadn't known. From the first moment He set His foot inside Simon's home, He was made to feel that He was, after all, nothing more than a lowly carpenter, that He should consider Himself lucky to be able to dine among the high and the mighty. Consequently, He was denied the common courtesy, prevalent at that time, of having His feet washed at the front door and the embrace of His host in the vestibule. Jesus accepted the insult silently and went to the place reserved for Him, the lowest place at the table, incidentally. The meal began, conversation was made, ordinary questions and answers passed among them, discussions on the higher things in life – prices; but all the while the crowd had its eye on Jesus. Nothing happened. Simon began to feel a little uneasy. The great sport he had anticipated had turned up missing. The party was falling flat on its face.

Then, finally, there was some action; but not the kind they expected, nor the kind they had planned. A woman appeared on the scene! This party was strictly "stag" – but this was no ordinary woman. It was Mary Magdalen, the notorious sinner. She stood there – lovely, beautiful, dangerous – looking over the crowd. Her glance fell upon Jesus as He reclined at the table. She made her way through the gathering, heedless of the shocked exclamations of the assembled hypocrites, men who probably had helped her on her way to the gutter.

When she reached the Son of God, without saying a word, without explaining anything, without asking any questions, she threw herself in a welter of tears at His feet. With her tears she washed away the dust of the road from the feet of Christ. Removing a couple of pins, she let her luxuriant hair come cascading down, and with it she dried His feet. Then in a gesture that was typically and beautifully feminine, she took what she considered one of her finest treasures, an alabaster box of precious, costly perfume, and poured it over His feet, filling the room with its heady, intoxicating fragrance.

At this moment, in the eyes of the guests, Jesus of Nazareth was on trial. Either He knew who this woman was, or He did not. If He didn't, then He was not much of a prophet. If He did know her and permitted her to kiss His feet repeatedly as if the two of them were old friends, then He was not the moral giant He was supposed to be. One way or the other, the crowd figured here was a paralyzing, damning discovery. The imposter had at last been unmasked!

But Jesus knew their thoughts, their slimy implications. He had won the devotion of this sinful woman, no doubt of it. Now He would go after His pompous host. He said, "Simon, I have something to say to thee." "Master, speak," answered Simon. Jesus began, "A certain money-lender had two debtors; the one owed five hundred denarii, the other fifty. As they had no means of paying, he forgave them both. Which of them, therefore, will love him more?"

It was a curious question but one that Simon understood. He had on occasion forgiven his debtors, and he realized that the gratitude he received in return was proportionate to the amount of the debt that he wiped out. He could only answer in one way, "I suppose, to whom he forgave more." "Thou hast judged rightly," said Jesus.

Then His tone changed and He began to lay into Simon. "I came into thy house; thou gavest Me no water for My feet, but she has bathed My feet with tears, and has wiped them with her hair. Thou gavest Me no kiss; but she, from the moment she entered, has not ceased to kiss My feet. Thou didst not anoint My head with oil; but she has anointed My feet with ointment."

It was just as if Christ had said: "You think you are so great, Simon. You are supposed to be a big, cultured, polished man. Why, Simon, you are ignorant. You could not even show Me, as a guest, the most basic forms of courtesy. You insulted Me. You may look with disdain and feigned disgust upon this poor woman, you may consider her dirt;

but, mark you, you will never be the person she is. You will never measure up."

There was no questioning the truth of this in Simon's mind. Mary Magdalen had shown herself superior to him. He hung his head, shamed before his guests. But Christ was not finished. This beautiful but fallen woman loved Christ and her love would be publicly rewarded. There at a Pharisee's table Christ taught His central doctrine, the one great truth that lies at the root of the whole Christian ideal. Without it, Christianity is dead; with it, she stands alone, unique and sublime in all the world: the doctrine of the personal love of Christ for all men.

So He said, "Her sins . . . shall be forgiven her, because she has loved much." Magdalen had hit the very bottom, a past master in the art and craft of impurity. She bore the shame of her sins publicly, while all we are expected to do is bear the shame of our sins privately, within the isolation and darkness of a confessional. Nor was Christ concerned over the number and the gravity of her sins; it was enough that she was sorry, that she had forever put behind her a life of sin.

As for herself, in throwing off the bondage of sin, she found in her release new joy. It was easy to leave. She rose from the floor and left, her feet hardly touching the ground. She had come to Him with her sins and He had restored her. Nothing else mattered to her. The woman of the streets was now the happiest woman in the world. Because she had discovered that there can never be any such thing as true happiness until we throw ourselves with all our sins at the feet of Christ to let Him work within our hearts the magic of His eternal love.

20 DINNER FOR FIVE (THOUSAND)

Christ now had but a year to go until His death, and these were busy days for Him. For He was concentrating on that gigantic task of preparing twelve men, unlettered but not unenlightened, to carry on His work when He could no longer be with them. He was now sending these Twelve Apostles out on their first field trips. What they had learned from the Master, they were not to hoard for themselves; no, they were to pass on these treasures to all peoples and all nations. This first trip lasted about two weeks; when they returned, they gave a full report of their activities to Christ. And the enthusiasm in their voices told Him of their enthusiasm for His work.

These trips meant long hours of hard work for the Apostles. When they returned, Christ would invite them to "come apart into a desert place and rest a little." With the Master, they would try to slip away in the early dawn; they would drift, nonchalantly, down toward the lake. There, one by one, they would clamber into Peter's boat and head across the lake. But they were followed – by people who had heard the voice of Christ, and wanted to hear it again. Like fire the word spread – that the Master was on His way across the northern tip of the Lake of Galilee. And then the mob, determined not to lose Him, would start out on foot, skirting the northern shore.

Evidently the shoe-leather express made better time than the sailboat. For, when Christ and His Apostles touched the eastern shore to seek solitude, there were the people, more and more of them. They had walked about five miles – and there they were! Their hungry eyes, fixed on Christ, pleaded: "Tell us more. Fill our hearts. We are starved for truth."

Peter wanted to get rid of the mob right then. Selfish, devoted Peter, he wanted God all to himself. But he said nothing. Nor did Christ object. They came to hear Him speak, so He would speak. All day long He was among them. Finally, toward evening, some of the Apostles thought that they had better call it a day. "Send the crowds away," they advised, "so that they may go into the villages and farms roundabout and find lodging and provisions." But Christ, in order to test Philip (and probably He was a bit amused), asked, "Whence shall we buy bread that these may eat?" Here Philip missed his cue. He thought, even with the Master beside him, that money was necessary. He forgot about that divine power that had shown itself so many times before. Then Peter interrupted: "There is a young boy here who has five barley loaves and two fishes; but what are these among so many?" Sometimes the Apostles, like the rest of us, could be very, very stupid.

Christ, disregarding their blank looks, ordered them to seat the people on the grass. The Master wanted to make sure there was no confusing this miracle. We were to get all the details. In fact, of all His miracles, this is the only one that is mentioned by all four writers. There were no mistakes. He took the two fishes, which were small, like sardines, dried and salted, then the five loaves of bread, broke them, put pieces into each Apostle's satchel, and sent them among the crowd.

Soon the truth of what was going on struck these incredulous men. They kept reaching down into their satchels and kept bringing food out in their hand. Then in order that the details might still be definitely recorded, Christ made them gather up what was left after the crowd had eaten, and they filled twelve baskets. Talk about a detailed miracle, this was it! And the mob, well fed and highly enthusiastic, tried to proclaim Christ king. This is what chased Him. He hustled His Apostles off into the boat and fled into the mountain to pray.

For the moment, He had driven home His point. The absolute, factual miracle of the multiplication of the loaves and fishes (no gimmicks involved, no tricks, but an open miracle for all to see) proved to anyone with reason that He was God. And this great miracle was deliberately planned in order to set up His first teaching on the Holy Eucharist. The Apostles saw the miracle. If Christ could do this, He could do anything! They were, therefore, in the best possible position to accept His teaching on the Eucharist.

So the next day, the crowd found Him back again on the other side of the lake, at Capharnaum. They complained because He had slipped away from them. They wanted Him because He had filled their "tummies," not because He had worked a great miracle. And He told them as much. But they asked Him, "What are we to do in order that we may perform the works of God?" To which question, He demanded that they believe in Him, that they stop asking for signs like the manna that fell in the desert in the time of Moses. He drilled home again the same old story, "Faith in Christ is the only way to please God." The basic act of man in his relations with God is faith. Christ knew that without their faith in Him, they (as well as ourselves) would never come to an understanding of, and a belief in, the Holy Eucharist. If they believed in Him, then they would have to accept the teaching of His Body and Blood. So He gave It to them.

"I am the bread of life. He who comes to Me shall not hunger; and he who believeth in Me shall never thirst. . . . I have come down from heaven." Here the crowd murmured its unbelief, "Who does He think He is? Is not this the son of Joseph whose father and mother we know? What's all this chatter He's giving us about coming down from heaven?"

But the Master silenced them, "Do not murmur among yourselves. . . . I am the living bread that has come down from heaven. If anyone eat of this bread he shall live forever; and the bread that I will give is My flesh for the life of the world."

There was no questioning this. Those who would say that the Eucharist is only a symbol of His Body have but to remember His words, ". . . the bread that I will give is My flesh." Nor need anyone try to say that Christ meant something else. He meant what He said and He said what He meant. There is no sane reason to question the true presence of Christ in the Blessed Sacrament.

"He who eats My flesh and drinks My blood has life everlasting and I will raise him up on the last day."

All these are strong words, indeed. But they are true! Granted, it is sometimes difficult for those of stingy faith to understand how Christ could exist in the Eucharist. We cannot understand how He multiplied the loaves and fishes; we cannot understand how He raised the dead to life. Many facts about Christ we cannot understand; but we know what He did. Just as truly as He cured the blind and the crippled, just as truly as He walked upon the waters, so He has also left Himself to dwell with us forever within the Holy Eucharist.

Probably we cannot comprehend it fully. It is too big for us. If we had a full understanding, we would never let a day go by without presenting ourselves at the railing to receive Him in Holy Communion. Our faith in Him is so weak. We walk into our churches, proud and haughty, but if we fully realized that He is physically present in the tabernacle, we wouldn't walk into a church. We would crawl in. And we'd go up the middle aisle on our hands and knees, knowing that as long as we received Him worthily, we would never really die. We would stop breathing and look dead. But actually, there would be no blackness at death. Only a new glorious light that would greet us in eternity.

People didn't believe Him then, and they still don't believe Him. But that doesn't matter. Each morning that we rereceive Christ, we make ourselves one with Him, we become almost like little gods ourselves. And we take Him into the world with us, hoping that some of His love and beauty will rub off on the people we meet in the course of the day. With Christ in Holy Communion we are able to make the world better; but most of all, by receiving Him, we make ourselves ready to receive someday the fruits of His promise, "He who eats My flesh and drinks My blood has life everlasting and I will raise him up on the last day." It is wonderful to know that, because of Christ, we will never experience death; we will never die!

21 ❦ THE WOMAN WHO WAS CAUGHT

The Feast of the Tabernacles, one of the great festivals in the Jewish year, brought people from nearly every corner of the then known land to Jerusalem. Staged late in September or early October, it was a gay and popular event, a religious feast which marked the end of the harvest and commemorated the ancient sojourn in the desert. Even as today, with people coming from far and near to conventions, and hotels not able to accommodate thousands of tourists, so it was in Jerusalem at the time of the Feast of Tabernacles. The people at that time would build little green huts of branches all over the squares and terraces of the holy city. And then, even as today, some of those who came would forget that it was a religious feast they had come to celebrate. Too often then, as now, morality went out the window, as "wine, women, and song" took the stage. The roistering, the looseness of some tended to spoil the religious aspect of the feast – and out of this, as might be expected, there was introduced into world history the incident known as "the woman caught in adultery."

This was the setting for one of the most celebrated and most beautiful episodes in the recorded life of Christ. However, if some of the early scribes had had their way about it, the account of this woman would have gone into the wastebasket. Some of the early Christians, suffering from a severe case of scrupulous delicacy, would have preferred to keep Christ aloof from any contact with such base carryings-on. Again, they tried to smother the story entirely, lest the people get the idea that Christ did not think adulteresses were so bad after all. The whole approach, of course, is plainly ridiculous. When Christ told the woman to "go and sin no more," He was not approving her shady morals. He was only forgiving her sins.

Jesus was teaching in the Court of the Women sometime during the feast when He was interrupted by a commotion; the Pharisees were at it again. They came bursting through the crowd, dragging a weeping woman by the scruff of the neck. When they had shouldered their way to the front of the crowd, they flung the woman out into the empty space before Christ. Disheveled and covering her face with her hands in shame, she sank to the ground like a bundle of rags.

The Pharisees who brought her were typical – genuine 14-carat phonies. Outwardly they were putting on a big show of holy righteousness; inwardly they were up to their old tricks – trying to make Christ lose face before the people. Unmoved by the pathetic picture of the poor sniveling female on the ground, they said to Christ, "Master, this woman has just now been caught in adultery. And in the Law Moses commanded us to stone such persons. What, therefore, dost Thou say?" Her smug, pompous, self-righteous accusers persisted.

In the backs of their puny, twisted minds they had devised (they thought) the master plan to trip up the Saviour. They had put Him (they thought) on the horns of a dilemma; in such position, that, regardless of which choice He made, it would be the wrong one. The woman had been caught. (Her partner in sin, as usually happens, had apparently managed to escape – the world is hard on women!) She could not deny her crime, so she must be punished according to the Law. In the Old Testament, Moses commanded that such persons be stoned. But now, what does the Master think? How should the culprit be treated?

The idea was this. If Christ spoke out in the woman's defense, He would stand self-confessed as a revolutionary, an enemy of the public welfare, and a destroyer of the Mosaic Law. If, on the other hand, He upheld the Law and encouraged these men to carry out the execution, then He would lose His hold over the people whom He had won particularly by His precepts of mercy and kindness. The Pharisees really thought they had Christ snowed. They waited for the fall of the Titan.

Jesus sat silently, using in a masterful way the dynamic pause. As He sat, He traced little signs in the sand. Some interpreters of Scripture have gone hog-wild over this little incident. Some said He wrote the names of sinful women who happened to be at present quite chummy with these particular Pharisees. Others surmise that He wrote the secret sins of the accusers upon the sand for the whole world to see. Either assumption would, it is true, be sufficient cause for these hypocrites to slip away into the obscurity of the crowd. But in heaven we will probably find out that Christ was not writing anything at all. He was just doodling. He was pausing to build up tension and, in the taut silence of the crowd, making the Pharisees realize what utter fools they were.

It worked. It began to dawn on them that their plan was not so smart after all. They had no reason to ask Christ to pass judgment on her. That was their job. Publicly, they had made first-class jackasses out of themselves. In disgrace, they slunk away through the amused crowd. But what made them move all the faster were the only words that Christ spoke, "Let him who is without sin among you be the first to cast a stone at her." These men who had traveled together, who had gotten drunk together, who had sinned together – all of them knew that there was not one lily-white character in the gang. The retort of Christ did indeed slam down the lid on their little conspiracy. In no time at all, they had disappeared.

Throughout the entire proceedings, the woman lay prostrate with her face in the ground, waiting for the first stone to strike. But it never did. Finally she looked up to find about her, not the men who were to murder her, but only the stones they had left behind them when they fled. Then she looked at Christ. He sat back, relaxed, and smiled at her – a tender smile, a smile of forgiveness. He looked about. "Has no one condemned thee?" He asked the woman. "No one, Lord," she answered in tears of repentance.

"Neither will I condemn thee. Go thy way, and from now on sin no more."

Jesus made a very interesting point here. He did not condone adultery, nor will He ever. But He did forgive it. Important, too, is the fact that Christ, while not minimizing the seriousness of sins against purity, did condemn in no uncertain terms the sin of hypocrisy.

A few months before this, a lawyer had asked Him, "What must I do to gain eternal life?" But He said to him, "What is written in the Law?" He answered saying, "Thou shalt love the Lord thy God with thy whole heart, and with thy whole soul, and with thy whole strength . . . and thy neighbor as thyself." And Jesus said, "Thou hast answered rightly; do this and thou shalt live."

It was here that Christ put love of God and love of neighbor on a par with each other, standing in such relationship that if we do not love one then we do not love the other. Practically speaking, if we harbor any kind of hatred in our hearts for anybody, then it's going to be impossible to love God perfectly. All of which is tough to take. But we must take it.

Unfortunately, impurity is rather rampant in the world today, gradually weakening in a most frightful manner the very structure of human society. To rise above it is a feat worthy of all praise, but it does not give us the right to look down our noses at those who never made it. Remember that they might have failed where we succeeded, only because their ideals and their goals were far higher than ours have ever been. There is every reason to hate sin but there is no excuse for hating a sinner. A sinful woman cowered at the feet of Christ; she is still with us. And society, with deep degrading hypocrisy, still stands with rocks ready. The greater evil is not in the woman who has failed, but in her smug, prissy, half-envious friends who turn their backs and leave her.

It is true that we do not know if Christ wrote the secret sins of the Pharisees in the sands of the Temple, but we do know that He will write our secret sins in the sands of eternity. And He will be merciful to us as long as we, in our lifetime, were merciful to those who failed simply because they never found the opportunities or the graces that we ourselves had found.

22 THE YOUTH WHO CHICKENED OUT

Many characters crossed the path of Christ while He was here on earth. Popping in and out of His life were kings and rulers, thieves and criminals, soldiers and children, farmers and politicians, even mothers-in-law. Some were good; others bad. Some knew Him intimately; others only casually. But whether much or little was written about them, all of them had been blessed with the glorious privilege of touching and hearing Christ. All of them saw God.

Among them was the rich young man. Christ had just left a dazzled group of little children and started down the road, when this particular young man put in his appearance. He was wealthy, well bred, and, in spite of his tender years, reckoned among the notables of the country. Basically good, he was a volunteer and a contributor to any worthy cause that came along, a born leader, known and beloved by all.

As Jesus passed by, he was swept up in the wild enthusiasm of the crowd; his heart was stirred to its roots. He had heard about this good Man Jesus, this Teacher who appealed to the nobler aspiration of men, who had made good people better and weak people strong. "Perhaps," thought the youth, "He will do something for me, offer me a special counsel." He elbowed his way through the crowd until he reached Jesus. There in the middle of the road he went down on one knee. He bore the stamp of loyalty, truth, and honesty; his dress was all that it should have been; his voice was mellow and warm. Christ was impressed. The boy said, “Good Master, what good work shall I do to have eternal life?”

Jesus answered, “If thou wilt enter into life, keep the Commandments.”

The young man was a wee bit deflated. “Keep the Commandments? Well, of course I do. Doesn't everybody? (He was that naïve, that good.) I ask this Man for meat and He gives me pabulum. But then, maybe He has some new commandments I haven't heard about. I will ask Him.” And he did.

The next statement of Christ was even more disconcerting than the first. “Thou shalt not kill. Thou shalt not commit adultery. Thou shalt not steal. Thou shalt not bear false witness. Thou shalt not defraud. Honor thy father and mother. Thou shalt love thy neighbor as thyself.”

“And this is all?” the young man thought. “Is this all He asks of me – only the basics? But I am finished with basics. My heart is on fire within me. I want to serve Him forever, to use my influence, my position, my wealth for the furthering of His cause. (He had his own ideas about serving Christ. What Christ wanted was not important.) I must convince Him of this.”

“Master, all these I have kept ever since I was a child. What is yet wanting to me?”

Christ looked right through the boy, and He liked what He saw – the swaggering heroism that throws caution to the winds, the treasury of limitless possibility, the boundless zeal showing through, and the sincerity. Whatever his first motives for detaining Christ might have been, they were genuine now. So something special is the result.

It is one of the rare incidents when an evangelist dares lay bare the thoughts and emotions of Christ. St. Mark says, "And Jesus, looking upon him, loved him." No question then as to where they stood. Now the Master must put the young man's love to the test. It is one thing to say, "I love God"; it is something entirely different to prove it. This young man would be given a chance to prove what he said. He had asked for more. Very well, Christ would give him more. Christ would offer him a special niche in the kingdom of heaven, if he wanted it. If he was big enough.

"And He said to him, 'One thing is lacking to thee; go, sell whatever thou hast, and give to the poor, and thou shalt have treasure in heaven; and come, follow Me.'"

The young man had asked for it. He had flung a big challenge at Christ; now he received a big answer in return. He had wanted to do something more, so he got more; more, in fact, than he had ever expected. He was offered immortality. He received a personal invitation to join the band of Apostles, to fill in the place that would be left vacant by the defection of Judas. He was given the opportunity to rocket into the big time, to get in on the ground floor of a big deal for eternity.

Too bad the whole thing fizzled. Too bad that, even so early in his life, he let himself become the slave of his shekels. Too bad that he was not poor, because the very thing with which he had hoped to serve Christ was the thing that scrubbed him right out and dropped him back into the obscurity from which he came. Otherwise, the Gospels would have been written differently. He might have been a great Apostle; he might have been our patron saint. Wealth was his executioner. He had one ride on the merry-go-round of life and he missed the golden ring. As it is now, we don't even know his name.

The sequel was sad. With all his riches he had wanted to

be of service. Instead, he was asked to get rid of them. Waste them on the poor. Throw them away like dirt — these possessions that he valued more than a promise of eternal life itself. It just didn't figure; it just didn't make sense. The joy he had felt on the initial contact with Christ faded into nothing. Nature said that it was asking too much, that the price was too high. It was wrong to wreck his life, his happiness, and his power for good. He was too accustomed to his money and all the comforts that it could bring him. So he would hang onto it; let somebody else give away his money and follow Christ. After all, these words of Christ were not a command, just a suggestion. Yes, let somebody else do it.

The account closes: "But when the young man heard the saying, he went away sad, for he had great possessions." It is the story of a youth's choice of a state of life, and a very tragic tale at that. He knew his vocation but he rejected it.

Today, with the Church in the throes of an acute shortage of vocations, we can easily presume that there are still rich young men turning away from Christ. These, too, are tragedies. Modern tragedies. But they will find in time that the world which they chose, in preference to Christ, will someday crumble and turn to ashes in their mouths. Then they will realize what fools they have been.

Jesus let the young man go. Perhaps he eventually lived a good life, perhaps he did use his wealth for good; yet, as long as he lived, he would never forget those eyes that looked on him and loved him, the voice that begged for his friendship and his companionship. He would never forget these. The joy of a given moment would leave him, his heart would shiver, and, pulling his gold about him, he would try to convince himself that he really was happy after all. Yes,

Jesus let him go. As he walked into the crowd, the eyes of Christ followed him. They haunted him forever.

The only consolation that Christ had at the moment was the thought of countless thousands of other young men in future generations who would not turn away from Him. There would be others who, hearing His glorious invitation, "Come, follow Me," would heed it. They would leave the world and all they had. They would discover their vocation and clutch it to their hearts, and upon their young shoulders they would heft the burden of God's Church.

Then, like every other person who ever left all things to serve God in religion, they would find that in giving up all for God, they would give up nothing. They would become rich with the freedom with which only Christ could set them free – to walk across the arches of the world in a deathless, driving quest for the immortal souls of men.

23 ❦ THAT I MAY SEE

The thing that most people know about Jericho is that one day "its walls came tumbling down." What they don't know is that somebody built them up again.

Jericho was an oasis in the desert. It was also the second most important city in Palestine and equal in area to Jerusalem itself. Like Magdala, it was a toney town, a winter resort, and, like such places, famous for three things – fruits, flowers, and wild women.

It was the battlefield for the great building war that went on between Herod and his son Archelaus. Herod would build a mansion; Archelaus would build a bigger one. Herod would come back with a giant swimming pool fed with mountain water; Archelaus would turn around and build the last word in gymnasiums. The result of such a war could only be splendor. And so it was – a wonderful amphitheater, a great stadium, a city of cities. Briefly, it was plush.

Like the corner drugstore where all the stags gather before moving, in the safety of a group, to the local high school ankle shake, Jericho was the rallying point where everybody from the north assembled to make the last seventeen miles into Jerusalem together. Everybody went through Jericho, like everybody goes through Chicago. And Christ, coming from the north on His way to the Holy City for the last time, funneled Himself and His followers through Jericho.

But He didn't preach there. He never once preached in Jericho. Maybe He thought it was just a waste of time. On this occasion, as always, He kept moving right on through town, the crowd following Him – His Apostles, friends, former fans of John the Baptist who had now switched their loyalties to Jesus, the curious who were neither with Him nor against Him but just tagged along looking for some kind of excitement. The spies were there, too. The spies were always there.

The roadside was lined with loiterers, toads, "con men," free-loader vagrants, and beggars. And the beggars are of interest here.

Numbered among them were two blind men, one of them named Bartimaeus (Son of Timaeus). He had been there monopolizing the same spot for a long time; a veteran, master-beggar, who in blindness had honed his sense of hearing to a fine edge.

There was certainly nothing unusual about these two. Blind men were common and Scripture makes many comments about them. Even today blindness is prevalent in

Palestine. Heat, dust, and disease team up together to rob people of their sight. In the record, Christ cured blindness six times. So Bartimaeus and his blind buddy were quite in character as they lay there in the ditch, trying to analyze and evaluate the sounds of this particular crowd going by.

It was not the sound of a marriage procession; the absence of loud, professional lamentation excluded the possibility of a funeral. It did not have, either, the riotous sound of Herod and his mob on the move. It could only be a group of pilgrims on their way to Jerusalem. Yet, with the vision and the taste of his ears, Bartimaeus knew that this crowd, for some reason, was different. He was curious. So he reached out, grabbed the first shirttail going by, and asked, "What's going on?" The answer: "Jesus of Nazareth is passing by."

Now Bartimaeus had heard many stories about Jesus, the Wonder-Worker who loved everybody. So right on the spot he made up his mind. "If Jesus has done so much for other people, maybe He will do something for me. This Jesus is no ordinary man. When He gets closer, I will do two things. I will tell Him that I believe in Him. Then, if I dare, I will ask Him to cure me."

In the noisy crowd, Bartimaeus would be noisier. At what he thought was the proper time, he let out a blast that must have sounded like the slamming shut of the gates of hell, "Jesus, Son of David, have mercy on us."

The people nearby, their ears ringing from the blast, tried to silence him. The Gospels are so charitable. They put it this way: "And the multitudes that went before rebuked him that he should hold his peace." Which is a nice soft way of saying, "Bartimaeus, shut your big mouth." The crowd, having a big time of it, wanted no interference from creepy beggars. But the blind men were desperate.

Bartimaeus would not be deterred. He cried a second time, even louder, "Jesus, Son of David, have mercy on us."

His spirit of "never-say-die," his loud screaming, his complete bottom-of-the-pile desperation – all these things paid off for him. Christ stopped. And when Christ stopped, everybody stopped. In the immediate silence that followed, the words, "Have mercy on us," hung, reverberating, on the air.

Jesus turned toward the side of the road and with His eyes bored a hole through the crowd, separated it, and there lay Bartimaeus, exposed. The Saviour spoke a quiet invitation and the crowd relayed it. "Arise," they said, "He calleth thee."

The blind men needed no second invitation. They struggled to their feet, threw aside the old rag that had been covering them as a protection from the dust of the road, and then, with arms outstretched, stumbling, groping, whimpering, they moved in their darkness toward the Son of God. Trembling with hope and aided by some of the crowd, they fell at the Lord's feet, their sightless eyes lifted toward the face of Jesus.

Jesus had always been especially considerate toward the blind, but these two really gripped Him. The visioned people standing around had referred to Him as Jesus of Nazareth. They still hung that insulting title, "Nazareth," on the end of His name. But the blind men had not cried "Jesus of Nazareth," but rather, "Jesus, Son of David." They gave Him His royal title. They were bigger than the crowd. And Jesus did not let this point pass unnoticed. Their tender faith would be rewarded. He knew what these poor wretches wanted, but He loved to be asked – He still does. He asked, "What wilt thou that I do to thee?" It was just as if Christ had said, "What do you want? Name it and it's yours. For I am God."

Bartimaeus could have asked for the world. He could have asked for his weight in precious gems or gold. But he, far wiser than we, because of his affliction, knew what the great treasure was. Not gold or glory; but something the rest of us take for granted. Daring everything, but with complete faith, he went way out on a limb by asking the impossible, begging for the one most precious thing of all – "O Lord, that we may see." He did not forget his buddy.

The face of Christ changed. Before this, He had been gaunt and drawn from lack of sleep and the thought of what lay ahead of Him in Jerusalem within the coming weeks. Now, noticeably, His face softened. Others would deny Him; but these two poor beggared blind men believed and trusted Him. And that was enough. They had knocked on the door of His heart and He would answer them. So He bent down as they crouched before Him; His fingers touched their sunken eyelids. He said, "Receive thy sight. Thy faith hath made thee whole."

And the blind men of Jericho opened their eyes now filled with the light of life, and they saw for the first time, standing before them, the Light of the World. "And they followed Him on the way, glorifying God." They followed Him forever.

Our blessed Lord did not cure these men simply because He was sorry for them. Nor was He trying to raise His stock in the eyes of the people. He was teaching them something, using this miracle to convey His readiness to give light to those who stumble through life with far greater affliction than physical blindness, namely, spiritual blindness. For the great blindness of the world today does not come from sightless *eyes,* but from sightless *souls.*

Worldliness and sensuality have thrown a stifling blanket around our souls. They have trammeled our awareness of the horror of sin. We just do not *see* the danger of sin. We do not *see* how much we stand to lose by our spiritual blindness. The condition of a world, fallen in many instances to the level of beasts, has come about, not so much because we are evil, but because we are blind.

Bartimaeus at least *knew* he was blind. We do not. So his prayer should be our prayer. Like him we should beg, not for the treasures of life, but rather for the treasures of soul, "O Lord, that I might see."

24 ❦ HOSANNA!

Jesus spent Saturday night with thousands of pilgrims under the stars, just outside the squalid little village of Bethpage (House of Figs). In the morning, and a historical Sunday morning it was, Christ looked down toward the village, noticed it was already astir, then called two of His disciples to Him. They were to go on an errand.

"Go into the village," He told them, "and immediately you will find an ass tied, and a colt with her; loose them and bring them to Me." While the disciples were trying to figure this out, Christ satisfied them by continuing, "And if anyone say anything to you, you shall say that the Lord has need of them."

Something was in the air. The Master was acting strangely. He was taking over completely. In truth, now He was the King of the Jews. Something momentous was about to happen; a phase in His life was about to begin. But only later would the disciples see in all this, and in what was to follow, a fulfillment of the prophecies.

The two disciples were not long gone when they came to the fork in the road and saw an ass and its colt tethered to a pole. There was no "For Hire" sign stuck in the ground beside them, for it was quite obvious that they were in the business of hauling tired pilgrims up over Mount Olivet and down into the Holy City. The owner was off in the distance somewhere, in the carelessness so common in the East. The disciples, nervously eyeballing the situation and wondering if they might be accused of appropriating a couple of hot donkeys for the Master, untied the animals and started back. The owner came out of nowhere like a cannon ball and there was a big Jewish rumble on the trail. Finally, the disciples said what they were supposed to say in the first place, "The Master has need of them," and the owner was only too happy to be of service to Christ. He charged nothing, which proved the enormity of his respect for the master.

The procession really began in Bethania, a city about five miles from Jerusalem. The whole town was bubbling with enthusiasm. The arrival of Jesus had reawakened all the excitement that was caused when He had called Lazarus forth from the dead only two months before. A fever had caught the people. If Jesus was going into Jerusalem, then they were going with Him. Furthermore, if He was going to ride over to Mount Olivet, then He was going to ride over in style. They rushed into their homes, grabbed up the finest garments they could find, and threw them over the backs of the little animals. Jesus mounted again, someone took the bridle, and off they went in glory.

The animal upon which Jesus sat was not some little mangy donkey that looked as if it had just stepped out of a sputnik. The robust and agile ass of the Orient is, even today, bright eyed and proud of carriage. It had no resemblance to its degraded relative in this country, the undernourished, ill-groomed, and unmovable American donkey. It was statelier and livelier; not the mount of a warrior, true; but the very essence of refinement. And the reason for the two animals: the mother ass was there to make sure the baby ass did not grow frisky and try to throw Christ from its back.

The procession started on its way up the eastern slope

of Mount Olivet. For years Christ had been hounded and hunted; now the whole thing was out in the open. Now, in marching straight to His death on the cross for the salvation of the world, He made three points:

1. He affirmed His mission by a clear messianic action in fulfillment of the prophecy made by Zacharias: "Rejoice greatly . . . shout for joy. . . . Behold the King will come to thee, the Just and the Saviour. He is poor and riding on an ass."

2. He left an example of humility and meekness – not a warlike king armed to the jaws, but a peaceful King astride a peaceful animal.

3. He proclaimed, loudly and publicly, His Kingship. No more running from the crowds who would make Him king, as He had done in the past. This time He was not running.

The procession, lively at the beginning, began picking up momentum as it moved. Word went ahead that He was coming. Pilgrims, encamped on the slopes, came down to meet Him; pilgrims from the valley of the Kedron came up to worship Him; pilgrims streamed out of the city. The suspense of thousands of years was over; the Jews had found their King. The parade snowballed into hysteria. Men scrambled up trees that lined the road and threw the palm branches down to the people. Soon everybody was waving them and casting them upon the road. With mounting hysteria, the Jews began tearing off their coats to make a carpet upon the road for their King. It was a glorious spectacle.

Then the procession found its voice and in rolling, thundering tones came forth the cry, "Hosanna!" – which means "Save us" but is also an exclamation of joy – "Hosanna to the Son of David! Blessed is He! Blessed is the King who cometh in the name of the Lord" – the same prayer which is eternally recorded in the Sacrifice of the Mass. The King had come at last. And He was Jesus Christ.

By this time, the Pharisees knew He was coming, and they proceeded to get ulcers. Orders had been published that when Jesus showed up He was to be seized. But how to seize Christ under these circumstances? The best they could do was try to break up the show, to turn the mob. They appealed to Christ Himself – brazen, hypocritical men that they were. Like traffic cops they pleaded that in such a mob as this somebody might get hurt. Better to call the whole thing off. "Master," they cried, "rebuke Thy disciples." But Jesus answered them, "If these shall hold their peace, the stones shall cry out." Never had Jesus been so defiant as He was now.

When Christ reached the top of Mount Olivet and saw the Holy City of Jerusalem spread out at His feet, tears filled His eyes. As if speaking to the city itself, He said, "For the days shall come and thy enemies shall cast a trench about thee and beat thee flat to the ground. And they shall not leave in thee a stone upon a stone."

This prophecy was fulfilled forty years later when the Roman General Titus attacked the city. He built his own wall around the wall of the city so that no one could escape. What occurred was too horrible to record in detail. Surrounded by Romans, unable to get food, the people became cannibals. Then the Romans moved in. The city was found later twenty to forty feet beneath the level of the ground. When discovered, not one stone rested upon another.

The joyous mobs stormed into the city. The rulers, the high priests, and Pharisees were all at their wits' end. They beheld the triumphant throngs, and one Pharisee, unnamed, went down into history as having paid to Christ one of the highest accolades possible when he said, "Behold, the whole world is gone after Him."

Finally, in the Temple, the people, attracted to other things, hoarse from having shouted too long and too loud, drifted away. The enthusiasm died, the ass and the colt were claimed by the owner, and Jesus found Himself walking with His Twelve through the courts. The rulers, under the circumstances, felt it would be too dangerous to capture Him at this moment. The party was over; the guests had left.

One minute thousands upon thousands had been screaming for Him; the next minute, fickle crowd that it was, they were gone. And not one of them even thought to invite Him for dinner. But Christ had made His point. Publicly He proclaimed Himself King, and the people accepted Him as such. But He was not fooled. Nobody ever fooled Him. He knew people then as He does today. On Sunday they screamed "Hosanna" and threw palms and garments at His feet; come Friday the same crowd would scream "Crucify Him," and would watch His blood pour into the dirt.

Yet, He took the bad with the good. He had compassion on the people. He understood the gross stupidity and inconsistency of men. He pointed it out to us. He showed us what to expect. Life will cuddle you today and beat your brains out tomorrow. God alone will never change!

25 THE FIRST MASS

During the last week of His life, Christ spent His nights in Bethany and His days in Jerusalem, coming to grips with the souls of men. His preaching on Monday, Tuesday, and Wednesday was dynamic, hurried, as if He feared that His time would run out before He had said everything He wanted to say. Pity the poor souls who were too busy to take the time to listen to Him, for never did He speak before as He spoke now. One must die in order to triumph; to save one's life, one must lose it. "And I, if I be lifted up from the earth, will draw all men to Myself." Sadly, He knew that it was a losing battle. They still threw foolish, doubting questions at Him. The game was soon to be played out; He was about to die. But he still preached.

He cursed the fig tree, no doubt to prefigure the fate of the city. Referring to the killer Pharisees, He taught the parable of the murderous husbandmen. And in order that Rome would not be dragged into this, He gave His famous counsel, "Render to Caesar the things that are Caesar's [be good citizens] and to God the things that are God's [be good Catholics]." Also, at this time, He spoke of the destruction of the world and of men's reward. "Come ye, blessed of My Father, inherit the kingdom prepared for you from the foundation of the world."

Then it was Thursday. Somewhere, in some storeroom where such things were kept, His cross was waiting for Him. Judas, after interminable haggling, had set his price at thirty pieces of silver (about eighteen dollars). Pilate had read a report concerning a tumult that was being caused among the people by a Healer from Nazareth. And now, Jesus was beginning to taste the agony which He must soon suffer. Mentally, He was feeling the weight of the cross and the sting of the whips. So now, in His final hour, He would leave the world His finest gift.

Calling Peter and John, He sent them into town to prepare the Passover meal. "But where wilt Thou that we prepare?" they asked Him. Much as on Palm Sunday, Christ outlined the plan, "Behold as you go into the city, there shall meet you a certain man carrying a pitcher of water. Follow him into the house where he entereth." This, then, would be the place for preparing the paschal supper.

The Apostles went their way, probably a bit fuzzy about it all; but sure enough, they found the man with the water and latched onto him until he led them into the courtyard of a well-to-do citizen. There the Apostles confronted the owner with their problem: the Master needed a place to eat the Paschal supper. Naturally, the owner was delighted to have Christ share his home. He led Peter and John to the Upper Room, a place about twenty feet square, with the table and benches neatly arranged. He was quite accustomed to renting the room for the Paschal suppers each year; he was honored this year by having such a distinguished Guest. But he never realized that his supper room was to be the first church of Christianity.

The Apostles liked the setup. What they needed now was the lamb, the bread, and the bitter herbs. And the wine, of course. They would buy these items in the bazaar on the west side of town, or in the outer court of the temple. At the appointed hour for sacrifice, they attended the ceremony where the lamb was slain, then returned to the Upper Room, roasted the lamb, prepared the food, and set the place in final order. By late afternoon, everything was ready; so they went to the Master with the news of their prodigious success. Their mission was accomplished.

Jesus led them to the Paschal supper. St. John starts the whole thing off with a prologue (and a real beauty it is) by saying, "Jesus, knowing that His hour was come that He should pass out of this world to the Father, having loved His own who were in the world, He loved them unto the end."

They had no sooner reached the Upper Room when there was a bit of rumble about where everybody was going to sit. After some grumbling and a little shoving, they found themselves on couches – Peter and John on either side of Jesus. The meal commenced, but some die-hards still felt they should have higher places at the table. They were acting like overgrown kids, until Jesus, in an example of beautiful humility, took upon Himself the office of servant and went around washing the feet of His Apostles.

Finally, toward the end of the meal, with the second cup

of ritual wine about finished and the third ready to be poured, Jesus looked around at His Apostles. These were the men He had chosen and trained over an intense three years. Looking into their souls that night, watching them fight among themselves for the best place, He might have been discouraged at what He saw.

Judas had just left, presumably on an errand, but Jesus could not miss the mark of traitor in him. Christ knew that at that moment Judas was among his own, closing the deal, stuffing the shiney money into his wallet. Jesus looked at Peter, His rock, the man upon whom He would build His Church, the first Pope indeed; yet in the heart of Peter He saw denial. Here was the man who had said, "To whom shall we go, Lord, for Thou alone hast words of everlasting life?" Yet in a few hours he would be swearing that he had never even known Jesus.

And all the rest of them, sprawled about Him, fighting for position, self-seekers who even at that late hour were still waiting for the time when Christ would take over the country, free all the Jews from the yoke of Rome, and set them on thrones to rule over the tribes of Israel. Christ saw them all for what they were, and, wonder of wonders, He loved them.

So at one of the most solemn moments in the history of the world, there with His dearest friends around Him in the Upper Room, the Son of God began the first Mass. He took into His hands a flat, round, unleavened loaf of bread, blessed it, broke it, and handed it to His Apostles, saying, "Take and eat; this is My Body which is being given for you. Do this in remembrance of Me."

Then, after the final cup of wine had been poured, He took the chalice into His hands and, having given thanks to God, He made them all drink of it, saying, "All of you drink this. This is the chalice of My Blood which is being shed for many."

This Last Supper, joined with His approaching death on a cross, is what we hold and treasure as the Sacrifice of the Mass. Each time Mass is offered, it is not a new sacrifice, or another sacrifice, but the continuation of the Sacrifice of Calvary.

For Christ still walks every road, climbs every hill, dies each day through His Mystical Body. And the great tragedy here is not that the world hates Him and rejects Him; the great tragedy here is that those who should be His friends are the ones who kneel each Sunday in their churches, bored to death over the whole thing. In the face of God's love, this boredom, this ingratitude seems an even greater mystery than the Sacrifice of the Mass itself.

26 THE LAST WORD

The supper was over. The fourth cup of ritual wine had been drunk. The grace after meals had been said. Now, according to custom, they lingered in their places a while and engaged in some quiet, leisurely discussion. It was there, in the midst of this relaxed atmosphere, that Jesus again jolted His Apostles. He said, "You will all be scandalized this night because of Me; for it is written, 'I will smite the shepherd and the sheep of the flock will be scattered.' But after I have risen, I will go before you into Galilee."

This was another of those dark forebodings that always disturbed them so much. Impatience spread across the face of the impulsive Peter. Jesus said to Him, "Simon, Simon, behold Satan has desired to have thee that he may sift thee as wheat. But I have prayed for thee that thy faith may not fail; and do thou, when once thou hast turned again, strengthen thy brethren."

The big fisherman did not like this at all. He loved Jesus with all his heart; and, Satan or not, he would never do anything against Jesus that would put him in a position where he would be forced to "turn again." He resented quite deeply the aspersion that Christ had cast upon him. So he started talking.

Like so many of us, Peter did a lot of talking – which is not much of a trick when you figure that parakeets do it too. Standing, flailing his arms in the air, in his deep voice he sounded off, "Lord, with Thee I am ready to go both to prison and to death. Even though all shall be scandalized because of Thee, I will never be scandalized."

It sounded good but, after all, it was only talk. Talkers seldom do anything. They just talk. So Jesus answered Peter, "Amen, I say to thee that this very night before a cock crows twice, thou wilt deny Me thrice."

This was more than Peter could take. He exploded into a torrent of screams and protests. Mark tries to put the hush on the thing by simply saying, "Peter went on speaking more vehemently." Suffice it to say that if the actions of Peter had been as big as his words, no soldier, no priest, no Pharisee would have laid a hand on Jesus. Actually they laid more than a hand on Him. Because, as you can see, the Apostles at that time, especially Peter, were just talk-talkers.

Finally, however, Jesus subdued their rantings. Before their peaceful supper became a complete bust, He opened His mouth to speak again. His words always put the silencer on them, and He still had something very important to say before He took His last departure. What He said then has since been referred to as Jesus' Last Discourse.

It was His farewell speech, not only to His faithful Eleven (Judas had since gone), but to His Mother, His friends in Bethany, and to all those, born and unborn, who would love Him and keep His ways. What He said is impossible to clarify, impossible to summarize; it is far too superior to be subjected to the stupid commentaries of stupid men. His words were an unconfined, unchanneled torrent of love – love for His Father in heaven, love for His disciples on earth. Although this final talk of His reached out to the heights of heaven, it never lifted itself from the bedrock of human society. It contained a clear picture of the brand-new world He had labored to build. It was without peer in all history. It brought into existence a new concept of life.

"A new commandment I give you that you love one another; that as I have loved you, you love one another. By this will all men know that you are My disciples, that you have love for one another." This was the force by which Christ would unite the world.

In those Grecian-Roman times, religions of the world, including ancient Jewry, always had some feature or motto by which they distinguished themselves from all others. The Pharisees, for example, were distinguished for their knowledge of "Tradition"; the Pythagoreans, by their knowledge of numbers; but the mark of the disciples of Jesus was to be the knowledge and the practice of love. Hence, He called his precept a "new commandment," because no founder of any society before Him had ever thought of giving his discovery such a unique identity.

Rome had given to the world her creations of force and law. Greece had given beauty and wisdom. The Orient had begotten strong mystical influences. But no one had as yet introduced love as a social force; because love, taken in its broadest sense to mean charity, had not yet been invented. Yet, from this day on, human society would reckon with this new force, invented and introduced by Jesus; and true human progress would be measured according to the completeness with which the law of love would be accepted.

Jesus spoke further. The Apostles, enraptured, tried to grope their way through these magnificent concepts as through some luminous mist.

"If you love Me, keep My commandments. He who has My commandments and keeps them, he it is who loves Me." None of this "faith alone is necessary" nonsense. Love of God had to be proved by works. None of this "I have God in my heart" stuff. Love of God had to be shown by the observance of His Commandments.

"Let not your heart be troubled. You believe in God, believe also in Me." He foresaw the fears and the burdens that we would have to carry in life, so He lifted us up by telling us how much He understood these things.

"In My Father's house there are many mansions. I go to prepare a place for you." He knew that many times in our lives we would falter in our awareness of heaven – life is so real and many times so bitter. So he told us about our future. He told us what to expect.

Then He prepared us for what was to come, so that we need never be surprised at martyrdom and persecution. "If the world hates you, know that it has hated Me before you. Yes, the hour is coming for everyone who kills you to think that he is offering worship to God. In the world you will have affliction. But take courage. I have overcome the world.

"Greater love than this hath no man that a man lay down his life for his friends. . . . Arise, let us go."

His discourse was ended. The Apostles followed Him out the door and into the night. They were thoroughly chastened men, cowered at all they had heard, scarcely able to believe it, but sure in the knowledge that it was true. Yes, they followed Him out into the darkness. But not for long. He was on His way to Calvary. It proved too much for them because that's the kind of people they were. They dropped off, afraid and ashamed. John, alone, went the whole way with Him.

27 THE PRISONER WAS FRAMED

When Christ and His Apostles left the Upper Room, they moved in silence along the southeastern section of the city on their way to the Garden of Olives. The Apostles were silent because they were too shaken up from the mystery of the Last Supper to say anything. Jesus was silent because He was afraid. The weight of the world's sins rested on His back. He was walking His last mile.

The group moved over the bridge of the Cedron (which in Hebrew means dirty or dark) and found themselves in a part of the city called "Gethsemani" or "oil press." It is most probable that the place was planted with olive trees and that it contained a stone press for the manufacture of olive oil. This was their little rendezvous where at times they gathered to get away from it all or just to rest.

He left His men at the opening of the garden but He took Peter, James, and John farther in. He wanted these three with Him in His hour of loneliness. He needed their comfort and their support. "Stay here and watch with Me," He said.

They watched, all right! They fell asleep just as soon as they sat down. In no time at all they were doing what most of us would have been doing under the circumstances. Jesus was suffering from what medical science calls *heratidrosis.* He was sweating blood. It is a condition brought on by severe stress or strain, and in the case of Jesus the condition was brought on by the thought of the agony before Him, and the feeling of the wave of fear and horror that swept over Him. He was enduring all this – and the Apostles were snoring. Jesus was praying, "Father, if Thou wilt, remove this chalice from Me" – and the Apostles were asleep.

Throughout this scene we cannot help being deeply conscious of the human nature of Christ. He was a young man, in His early thirties, and death was closing in on Him. He could smell death. Taste it. And He would not have been human if His flesh did not crawl and quake at the thought of the kind of death He must die. His heart was heavy, His consciousness so distraught that He asked His Father for a miracle, which would naturally have torn down everything that He had come this far to do. This is, indeed, the beautiful human Christ, who would not call upon His divinity to shield Him from the wrath of men.

This incident alone bears out the truth of the Gospels. For if the Gospels were not true, if the Gospels were a fabrication or an invention of some ancient writer, then they would never have mentioned anything like this, an incident so degrading to a God. The fact that it is written down by Matthew, Mark, and Luke bears witness to its truth. In fact, it puts the stamp of truth on everything these men wrote.

Finally, when His prayers were finished, Jesus awakened the three who were near Him, and He must have broken their hearts by the pathetic question, "Couldst thou not watch one hour with Me?" He did not wait for an answer. None was necessary. He simply said, "Rise, let us go; behold, he is at hand who will betray Me."

Indeed, he was. Judas, his bag of silver coins jangling at his belt, led a group of Jews with burning torches into the garden. They came armed with swords and cudgels to take the Prince of Peace. Judas had his work cut out for him. He told the temple servants and the soldiers that there would probably be a crowd around Jesus. There must not be any blunders. "Whomsoever I shall kiss, that is He; hold Him fast."

True to the plan, Judas walked up to Christ, raised himself on his tiptoes, and kissed the Son of God upon the cheek – the world's greatest act of betrayal by the man with the blackest soul. The soldiers moved with dispatch. They seized Jesus, bound His hands, and led Him away.

The Apostles, of course, were stunned by the swiftness and the unreality of it all. They had seen their Master, the Invincible One, tied up and surrounded by armed men. They had seen the cruel faces of the Jews. And they "chickened out." They fled the garden in panic. Now at last they knew how weak was their love for Christ. They must have hated themselves as they ran. But they ran just the same.

Christ was first and immediately taken to Annas, an old man who had held the office of high priest for seven years until he got kicked out. But he had great wealth and powerful influence. That is why his five sons and his one son-in-law succeeded him to the office. Just how good a high priest he was can best be learned from the historian Josephus who said of Annas, "None was so astute as he in enriching himself." No, he did not hold office, but nothing was done without first consulting him. He said nothing to Jesus; he only ordered that the Prisoner be brought to Caiphas, his son-in-law.

Caiphas, who lived just across the courtyard from Annas, was a vulgar career man, afraid of what people might say about him, afraid of losing his job. And right now this Man before him constituted a real threat. As far as he was concerned, this Jesus had to go. He questioned the Prisoner, hoping to get some admission of guilt that would make the trial on the following morning a mere routine. One thing was sure in the mind of Caiphas – guilty or not, this Jesus was a dead man. And while Jesus was suffering the humility of being grilled by this man, His own beloved Peter was saying with curses, "I know not this Man of whom you speak."

It was in the house of Caiphas that Jesus spent that long last Thursday night. His captors gave Him no rest, but sank to the lowest depths of brutality in their treatment. They spat in His face and insulted Him. Right here we might pause to wonder what these executioners said when the tables were turned in eternity, when they were the prisoners of God. What excuses did they give to Christ?

Early Friday morning, the Great Council of the Jews assembled. It was called the Sanhedrin. Caiphas presided. The thing was fixed. It was a rigged jury and a rigged trial. Vagrants and bums, who would do anything for a buck, filed in to tell some trumped-up stories concerning what Christ had said about destroying the Temple. They got their lines twisted; they contradicted themselves. Finally, Caiphas, realizing that the whole thing was getting ridiculous, decided on a bold move that would go to the root of the matter. He arose and asked of Jesus, "Art Thou the Christ, the Son of the Living God?"

There was absolute silence throughout the great hall. The Sanhedrin sat straight and still, like plaster statues. The whole world waited. And the answer came strong and crystal clear, "I am."

Christ drove the last nail into His cross when He said that, but it was good news for us. Now we know for certain who He is: the Son of the Living God. Any doubts that we might have fostered, in the face of His capture and subsequent humiliation in the hands of temple servants, disappear. Now we know who He is. And we need never doubt again.

As for Caiphas, this is what he was waiting for and, ham that he was, he went into his act. Like a maniac, he rent his garments; that is, he tore his robe from the neck down to the belt. He screamed, "What further need have we of witnesses? You have heard the blasphemy. What think you?" And they said in answer, "He is guilty of death." So the verdict was given, and Jesus was condemned to die. The only thing they needed was the consent of the Roman Governor.

Thus was rung onto the stage of life the great enigma, Pontius Pilate, a sometimes heroic, sometimes spineless man who almost became the champion of the day, yet left the mark of coward upon his name. He was a good man as pagans go, and he had no love for the Jewish leaders. Pilate was for anything or anybody that the Jewish rulers were against. The Jews were against Christ. Automatically, and in heart, Pilate was on the side of Christ.

Too bad Pilate could not have stuck to his guns. Instead, like all the others, he shared the guilt of the murder of Christ. Like all others, he wanted to save his job. He placed his loyalties with the kings of earth, and let the King of Heaven stand condemned before him. Like all such politicians before and since, he smothered his conscience and covered his eyes because the price that he would have been forced to pay for what was right was just too high for him. He chose the world, in preference to Christ.

28 ❦ WOMEN, 4 TO 1

We read it time and time again in the Gospels: ". . . and the multitudes followed Him" – which means a lot of people knew Christ was around. They listened when He spoke, they watched when He healed the sick, they were among the thousands that He fed on the hillside. Mobs of people tried to make Him their King. Jam-packed crowds cried out, "Hosanna to the Son of David!" on Palm Sunday. All in all, men, women, and children without number passed through His life, and loved Him in the passing, for He was so lovable in Himself.

But now, in the twilight of His life, the sentence of death slapped upon Him, the impending agony of crucifixion hanging over Him, our only question is: "Where in the world are His friends?"

Where are the lepers He cleansed? The blind men to whom He gave sight? The cripples whom He healed? They owe Him something. But maybe we had better not look for them, because, if we do, we might find them in the middle of that swollen mob, screaming for His blood, or off in the darkness hiding for fear that in sharing in His generosity they would automatically be expected to share in His shame. People are funny. Those whom we would expect to make some effort to free Him from His bondage just aren't around now. They do not know Him. They do not know anything. They are keeping their mouths shut.

All right, so that's the way people are. But why do the closest friends of Jesus have to act like the rest, as though they never even knew Him? It is a hard thing to understand. The only saving feature in the whole pathetic episode – the women.

Men, of course, have been considered from time immemorial the stronger sex; and women, bless them, the weaker. Maybe this is true. But the last day of Christ's life certainly puts the lie to this line of pompous masculine thinking. We have only to read the accounts of His passion and death to realize who stayed with Him and who did not. The men friends of Jesus, with the exception of John, ran to save their hides; but the women – they not only refused to run away, they made sure that the world knew just how they felt about the Master.

Take the man, Judas, for instance. He was an Apostle, had followed Jesus for three years, had sat at His feet; he was so special, in fact, that he was entrusted with the care of the little money they had. What a disappointment he turned out to be! He was a schemer who hit upon a brilliant idea to turn a fast buck. He would play the stool pigeon. He would sell Jesus for a price, pocket the bread, then sit quietly by, as Jesus again escaped His enemies.

That's what he thought! Yet, as the trial wore on, he saw that the Master whom he had betrayed was really going to die. He just fell apart. The results of his chiseling were far different from what he had expected. All of a sudden he realized the abysmal injustice he had committed, and his love for Jesus destroyed all his other loves, especially that of money; but it was a crippled love that could not rise to ask forgiveness. The thirty shekels began to feel like hot coals in his pocket. This money, which he had thought would satisfy his hunger, became a thing of intolerable bitterness to him. It branded him with the mark of the traitor. So he would dump the evidence. Running in among the smirking priests, he screamed, "I have sinned in betraying innocent blood." And he tried to give the money back. They spurned him. "What is that to us?" they answered. "This is your problem now, you juggle it. We fulfilled our bargain; what you do about it is your business."

Judas went mad. He ran to the "holy place" and flung the coins to the floor. His heart was so hardened now that he could not even think of asking for forgiveness. So in a fit of rage, he went out, got a stout rope — and hanged himself. The tree he chose was on the edge of a deep ravine, and the convulsive jerking of his body caused the limb to break, sending him down upon the jagged rocks below. Luke put it like this: "Judas, falling headlong, burst in the middle and all his bowels gushed forth." Maybe Judas was insane and therefore did not know what he was doing. Maybe in his last breath he cried out to God for mercy. Maybe his soul was saved. But as for Judas himself, what a failure his life was!

Peter was almost as bad. With all his boasting about how much he loved Christ, when things got hot he took to his heels with the rest of them. Oh, he did not run far; just far enough to make sure he wasn't being chased. Then, when he thought it was safe enough, he slunk back again, regained most of his composure, and proceeded to put his head in the lion's mouth. Some newsy woman spotted him and suggested that he was one of the disciples. Peter denied it, of course. Later on, she accused him again, this time in front of other people. He denied it again. Finally, he was accused a third time, and this time it was his tongue that gave him away, his Galilean accent which stood out in Jerusalem like the accent of a Bostonian in the Tennessee hills. And a third time he swore that he did not know Christ.

Then the cock crowed, and the sound hit Peter like a

hammer. At that very moment, Jesus passed through the court and, with one look, melted Peter's heart. Peter left the scene of his crime and went out and wept bitterly. Years later he proved himself by being crucified, head down, on a cross, but on the night when Christ really needed him and wanted him, he was a bitter failure. An object lesson to all of us is that even the great can fall; and when they fall, they make a really big noise. As for the rest of the Apostles, they did not even show their noses.

But the women! For them we can have nothing but admiration. Certainly we know that, at the foot of His cross, the women outnumbered the men, four to one. And on His way to Calvary, the so-called "Weeping Daughters of Jerusalem," a group of pious women dedicated to the works of charity, elbowed their way through the crowds of tramps, drunkards, pickpockets, thieves, and cutthroats, so that they might stand and publicly lament the great injustice of this evil day. They wept openly.

And for sheer beauty and militant love, we have the tradition of Veronica. We know her through the Stations of the Cross, but she receives no mention in Scripture. She is still real, she is still a woman in love with Christ.

Veronica knew Roman law. She knew that, according to that law, a prisoner on his way to death had no rights. He could be insulted but he could not be helped in any way. But Veronica did not give a hoot about Roman law. She knew where she was needed. So, as the dreary procession approached, she fought through the crowd that lined the street, ran out into the middle of the road, and, falling on her knees with a towel extended in her hands, she waited for Him, so that she could wipe the blood and sweat from His face.

Veronica was the only nurse Christ had. How much good

she did for Him is not the point. The point is that everybody knew where Veronica stood. Everybody knew whose side she was on.

Christ made many friends during His life; He also lost many at His death. If what Pascal says is true, that "Christ will be in His agony until the end of time," then we must make some kind of stand. Either we are a friend He made in His lifetime, or a friend He lost at His death.

If we're the kind of people who hide our faith for fear of what others might say about us, then we're the ones who ran from Christ then, and still run from Him today.

But if we make it a point of letting everyone we meet know just what we are, and if our affiliation with Him in His hour of deepest defeat is our proudest boast, then we have every right to stand within the circle of His "best" friends at the foot of His cross, to let the ocean of His precious blood pour down into the deepest recesses of our dry and empty, hungry souls.

29 BLOOD ON THE WHIPS

Jesus got a quick shuffle from all sides on the last day of His life. He was dragged from Annas to Caiphas, then to Pilate, to Herod, and back to Pilate again. They all knew that Christ was innocent, but they were shifty, each one trying to shift responsibility for the evil deed upon the next fellow. About the only thing we can say about these men is that they had a conscience. Too bad they didn't follow it. When they finally stopped playing pussy-in-the-corner and the game was over, it was Pilate who alone could have saved Christ's life. But he didn't, as we know so well.

Throughout most of this shuffling, Pilate was much concerned over putting justice before politics. Finally, fed up and afraid, his brains became screwed on sideways from confusion. In a last effort to find his way out of the maze, he forgot justice and played the politician. It was then that he made himself completely ridiculous. He wrote into the pages of history one of the greatest contradictions of all times. In a frantic effort to clear himself of guilt and with a hope of derailing the thundering persecution train, he said to the assembled crowds, "I find no cause in Him, therefore I will scourge Him and release Him." It was as logical to say, "This Man is innocent, therefore, like all innocent men, He must be whipped."

SS. Matthew, Mark, and John report the entire episode at the pillar in one line. St. Luke, the doctor, does not even mention it. Obviously, they could not bear to think about it, let alone write it down. Still, we all know what it was like. Several classical descriptions from ancient literature leave us no doubt of its horror. Suetonius and Livy show us sadistic magistrates exhorting those with the whips to strike harder; Cicero and Plutarch tell of victims falling dead, with blood streaming out of them, before the punishment was even finished.

Scourging has been practiced by the Jews from very ancient times for certain offenses, but the law demanded moderation in its use. Only an ordinary whip or rod could be used, and no more than forty lashes could be given. The usual procedure was to beat a man thirteen times on the back, thirteen times on the left shoulder and thirteen times on the right. Then there was no mistake about going over the allowable forty lashes. In Roman law, however, things were quite different. The number of lashes was not governed by any general law. It was determined by the decision of a judge, or subject to the whim of the executioner.

There were two instruments of torture in use. One was

the *flagella,* some leather thongs knotted at the end, or more commonly tipped with leaden nails. This thing, used with enormous force, could break a man's rib. It could certainly flay the skin right off the body. The other was the *flagra,* a whip made of iron chains. The scourging itself found the victim stripped and fastened to a stout, short post only a little more than two feet high so that there was no protection from the encircling scourges. Such a punishment among the Jews carried no special degradation, but among the Romans it was the lowest form of punishment, meted out only to slaves.

Certainly it is hard to visualize the true picture of Jesus bound to the post and subjected to this horrible form of punishment. The concepts of artists are far from realistic. Two drunken soldiers, either Syrians or Bedouins, tore at the body of Christ until their arms were tired from the exertion; then two others took their places. After a short while, Christ was reduced to a sickening and terrifying monstrosity. His neck, back, hips, arms, and legs grew livid, then became streaked with bluish welts and swollen bruises. Gradually the skin was lacerated, the blood vessels burst and blood spurted everywhere, until every one of His features was disfigured, and nothing was left but a bleeding mass of flesh.

According to sound medical diagnosis, no man could live through an ordeal like this. But Christ did. He took our sins upon Himself and paid the debt of their evil. He should have died there at the pillar, but He would not let Himself off that easily. He knew His job. Only His death on the cross would redeem us, the scourging was but a prelude. He had to stay alive at the pillar so that He would be able to die on the cross.

When the scourging was over, the soldiers took Jesus into

the palace. First they stripped Him and put a scarlet cloak of mockery around His shoulders. Then as an added contribution to His suffering, they placed upon His head a crown of thorns.

This crown was not really a headband as we see it so often depicted. It was a sort of cap made from thorny branches. It is generally admitted, too, that the crown was made from a thorn-bearing tree common in Judea. No doubt, there was a heap of these branches in the praetorium used for making fires by which the soldiers could warm themselves at night. One soldier might have stuck himself on a thorn while refueling the fire and got the bright idea of adding this further pain to Christ. The thorns were long and very sharp. And since any scalp bleeds easily, the wounds of Christ must have caused more loss of blood when the cap of thorns was driven against His head by violent blows from a stick.

It is rather difficult to believe this whole thing. Christ, who never hurt anybody, was being hurt by everybody. Innocence was never subjected to greater degradation. But the point is: He was not paying for His crimes (He had none); He was paying for ours! For every sin of impurity, He suffered the sting of the lash.

It is about time we started paying in some way for our own crimes by accepting the suffering and the pains that life throws in our way. Instead of asking ourselves why we must suffer, we should take the sufferings of the world in our arms as if we were entirely responsible for them. We can talk all we want about loving Christ, and we can read all we want about His crucifixion, but we still never really come to love or understand Him until we learn to suffer — not as an animal, but as a man.

Only by feeling our comparatively trifling pains can we

begin to understand in some small way the ordeal He went through for unworthy man. One thing is certain; no matter how tough we might have it in life, He knows about it. He loves us for it, because He went through it first.

30 THE WAY OF THE CROSS

Pilate asked the mob what they wanted him to do with Jesus, and the mob put him straight: "Crucify Him!"

If the Jews wanted to be consistent, they would have insisted that Christ be stoned, for that was the Jewish method of inflicting death on one guilty of blasphemy. But they were keeping this thing very Roman, and death by crucifixion was entirely the Roman way.

Rome, itself, always had a real terror of crucifixion. Cicero spoke of it as "the most cruel and atrocious of punishments; the extreme and worst punishment of slavery"; and later he said, "There is no epithet whatever which may fittingly describe a thing so infamous." Yet, horrible as it was, the Jews demanded the death of Jesus by crucifixion; and Pilate, finally overwhelmed, completely demolished, his every attempt to save Christ frustrated, at last gave in, washed his hands of all guilt (as if he could), and let the howling, hysterical Jews have their way. He just quit, and the wheels of crucifixion began to turn.

The cross on which Jesus was to die could have been any one of three types commonly used at the time. There was the regular cross called the *immissa;* there was a cross shaped like a capital T called the *commissa;* and a third one shaped like a capital X was called the *decussata* (slant-wise). The *immissa* was the one most probably used here. The vertical part of it was already planted on the top of Calvary; the crossbeam was carried by Jesus.

The procession began at the praetorium. A soldier on

horseback led the way, followed by a herald announcing the prisoner's crimes. The idea was to attract as many people as possible to see the condemned man, to heap insult on him as well as blows, and, incidentally, to learn the lesson of Rome's might and power.

After the herald came Jesus, dressed in His own garments and surrounded by four guards who were also His executioners. He still wore the crown of thorns, and carried around His neck a white board on which was written in three languages, Hebrew, Greek, and Latin: "Jesus of Nazareth, King of the Jews." Then the two robbers and their grim escort followed in single file. The multitude streamed along behind.

Ordinarily, the procession would have followed the main streets as an exhibition of justice, but, since the city was crowded with pilgrims from all lands, it took a short cut. Just outside the walls at the northern end of the city, there was a little rocky mound, a few yards higher than the surrounding territory, the appearance of which had prompted its name, "the skull," or in Latin, *Calvaria,* and in Aramaic, *Golgotha.* It was an ideal spot for crucifixion because its position guaranteed that the condemned man would be in full view, and since it was such a short distance from the city gate, many people were sure to pass that way. Besides, there was a tomb nearby, which made it quite convenient for the disposal of dead bodies.

The walk from the praetorium to Calvary could not have been too long because the next direct route to it was only a little over half a mile; but to Jesus, in His condition and carrying His cross, it must have seemed like a million miles. He tottered under the great weight and stumbled at every step. The possibility that He might fall, never to get up again, worried the captain in command. If the execution were delayed or incomplete, he would be severely reprimanded by his superior officers. Hence it was that Simon of Cyrene came into the picture. He was a farmer, in from the country, and he wanted nothing to do with all this; but he had no choice. He took the crossbeam from Jesus and followed Him up the hill.

When the procession reached the top of Calvary, the crucifixion was carried out immediately. Stripped of His garments, Jesus was laid on the ground. His arms were stretched along the crosspiece He had carried and His hands were nailed to it, the spikes being driven not through the palms of His hands but through His wrists. Then, with ropes, He was hauled up to the vertical beam and set astride the support. His feet were nailed. And so hung the Son of God upon His cross.

He looked down upon the crowds that surrounded Him and He must have been disappointed at what He saw. The executioners were there shaking dice for His clothes, the soldiers impatiently standing by, hoping for Him to die quickly so that they could return to their barracks; and the Pharisees, the priests, all screaming insults at Him: "If Thou are the Son of God, come down from the cross. He saved others; Himself He cannot save. If He is the King of Israel, let Him come down from the cross and we will believe Him." Then the people crowded the hill, curious like all people who gather about the scene of an accident, morbidly fascinated by the sight of blood. And yet, in the midst of all the hateful confusion, Jesus could see only a few friends – and most of them were women. Only John, of all the Twelve, stood openly and bravely at the foot of the cross.

In those final hours with His life's blood dripping surely away from Him, Jesus gave all the more generously to the world. First of all, as a shining example to all those who live their lives in seething hatred and revenge, He granted to His executioners and to all those responsible for His death, complete forgiveness: "Father, forgive them for they know not what they do."

Then to a desolate lonely thief who asked it of Him, Jesus gave the gift of salvation: "This day thou shalt be with Me in Paradise."

And finally, to all the world He gave one of His finest gifts, His own Mother: "Woman, behold thy son; behold thy Mother."

These were His parting gifts to the world. Now, feeling the current of God's wrath over the sins of the world, He cried out, "My God, why hast Thou forsaken Me?" He gasped, "I thirst." He proudly announced the finish of His work on earth, "It is consummated." Lastly, in the final moments of His life, He cried, "Father, into Thy hands I commend My spirit," to which St. John adds the final, glorious, bloody, and triumphant exit, "and bowing His head, He gave up the Spirit."

This is all history. This is all true. If Christ in His love gave so much to the world, we might try giving something back to Him. We might try putting into the world He loved a little love of our own.

31 A BORROWED GRAVE

The Son of God had no sooner bowed His head in death upon the cross than the tensions of nature snapped and many strange things happened in the darkened city. The first thing to be torn asunder was the heavy purple and gold veil that hung before that sacred enclosure known as the Holy of Holies. Under the Law, it could be parted only once a year; but now God wished it to be known that, through the merits of His Son, His sanctuary was thrown open to all mankind, "the ban and reproach wiped away."

Then the tremors of earthquake shook the earth: "The rocks were rent and the tombs were open, and many bodies of the saints who had fallen asleep arose; and coming forth out of the tombs after His resurrection, they came into the holy city and appeared to many." Even today a crack is still visible on Calvary. It is two feet long and one foot wide, and, contrary to the usual fissures produced by earthquakes, it does not follow the veining in the rock, but runs against it. In general, nature protested against the murder.

People were also affected. The commanding officer in charge of the execution had a complete change of heart. He had been won over by his Prisoner. Jesus was so different from the rest. Not with screams of violence and cursing had He gone to His death, but quietly as a lamb. And so it was that, after he had pierced the side of Christ with a lance, he turned his back on the cross and started toward the city, tears filling his eyes as he whispered over and over, "Truly, this was the Son of God."

Even the attitude of the mob had changed. A while before they had carried on like wild animals; now they were ashamed of themselves and returned to their homes, "beating their breasts." Yes, they had all changed; but wasn't it a little late?

Time was passing and the three condemned men must be put away before the Feast began. The soldiers broke the legs of the two thieves, hastening their death, but when they came to Jesus, He was already dead. So they picked up their things and went home.

In the meantime, Joseph of Arimathea, a wealthy man of great prestige, a member of the Sanhedrin and a secret disciple of Jesus, went to Pilate and asked permission to take the body of Christ from the cross and accord it fitting burial. When Pilate had been assured that Jesus was dead, he gladly gave him permission. His respect for Jesus, whom his weakness forced him to condemn, still lingered in his heart; and he was glad to know that Jesus would not be thrown into the common grave for the executed, along with the two thieves.

Joseph, with his friend Nicodemus, set about taking the body of Jesus down from the cross and preparing it for burial. Mary was at hand. She would not be denied the honor of receiving the dead body of her Son into her arms. The three of them, with the assistance of some of the pious women, prepared the body of Jesus for the grave, using spices and precious ointments, and then wrapped it entirely in a shroud of fine linen. Time prevented their moving the body to a tomb any distance away, but this problem was solved by the generosity of Joseph who offered his own, nearby.

This tomb, which Joseph freely gave to Jesus, was arranged on the inside with a vestibule and then a burial chamber with its niche for the body. The tomb was closed by a huge stone set against the opening. This stone was moved to the right or left along a little groove hewn out of the rock on either side of the door. But it took a lot of muscle to move it. Finally, since Jesus died about three in the afternoon, everything was over by six o'clock. Joseph, Nicodemus, and John rolled the stone into place at the entrance and departed.

It was a sad and lonely group that returned to the city, but there was great rejoicing among the triumphant Sanhedrin. It celebrated its Paschal supper with the traditional aid of gaiety, but with the extra satisfaction of having done a job on Jesus.

The Galilean Rabbi was dead, very dead indeed. They would never be forced again to listen to His denunciations. Never again would He humiliate them in the eyes of the people. At last they were secure. As for the disciples He had managed to attract, they would scatter now that their Master was dead. Soon His name would be gone from the minds of the people and no one would speak of Him any more. Everything had gone so well; theirs had been a splendid victory. How it must have added special flavor to their Paschal supper!

Yet, the more they thought about it, the more they began to notice a little flaw in the shining crystal of their cup of triumph. It was just a trivial matter, of course; but maybe they had better check on it. They recalled that while Jesus was still living, He had predicted that, three days after His death, He would rise again. This was sheer boasting on His part, they were sure of it. After all, they knew that the resurrection of this man from the grave was impossible. But, just in case, they thought they had better look into the matter.

So, on the following day, although it was their Pasch, some of them took the short, permissible walk to Pilate's house to give him some pertinent advice: "Sir, we have remembered how that deceiver said while He was yet alive, 'After three days I will rise again.' Give orders, therefore, that the tomb be guarded until the third day, or else His disciples may come and steal Him away and say to the people: 'He has risen from the dead'; and this last imposture will be worse than the first." Yes, they were smug ones, they were. And how they annoyed Pilate. But he still bent over backward for them.

He answered them, "Go, you have a guard. Guard it as well as you know how." So they went and made the sepulcher secure, sealing the stone, and setting the guard. In their petition to Pilate, the Sanhedrin gave testimony of Christ's claim to divinity. That was what they meant by "the first imposture," namely, that He claimed to be the

Messias. The last imposture referred to His resurrection. For the record, they left no doubt as to His death. They proved that He was still in the tomb on Saturday morning, for they sealed the door and posted the guard. He was, therefore, dead, buried, and guarded. No one could possibly steal away His body. The only one now who could move the body of Christ would be Christ Himself. The Pharisees went back to their homes, secure in the knowledge that they had prevented any hitch in their plans. They never realized that Divine Resurrection would shortly break through the seal that they had set upon the door of His tomb.

through the closed door and said to them, "Peace be to you." Thomas wasn't there. He still did not believe. So Jesus favored him with a special visit and a gentle rebuff by saying, "Blessed are they who have not seen and have believed."

Jesus stayed with them in Jerusalem and in Galilee, teaching them many wonderful things. Then, forty days after His resurrection, He gathered them about Him on the top of the Mount of Olives. What happened there is best described by St. Luke: "And it came to pass as He blessed them, that He parted from them and was carried up into heaven."

The Acts of the Apostles puts it this way: "He was lifted up before their eyes, and a cloud took Him out of their sight." Jesus had ascended into heaven; His work on earth was finished.

Up there He awaits our coming so that He might open to us the mansion that His Father has prepared for those who love Him. It is certainly worth waiting for. It is certainly worth working for. It is our heritage, our right.

Thus we leave Jesus as the greatest paradox in history. He spends His youth in isolation. For thirty years no one knows who He is except two or three persons who are as silent as He. But when He is thirty, He emerges into public life. He has no money, no weapons, no academic knowledge, no political support. He spends most of His time among the poor, and with particular solicitude seeks out publicans, harlots, and others rejected by society. He works miracles in great number and variety. He gathers a group of fishermen around Him. His activity lasts for three years. Then He is crucified.

But today He is more alive than ever among men. All have need of Him, either to love Him or to curse Him, for they cannot do without Him. No one cares any longer, one way or the other, about Caesar or Napoleon for they are gone. But not Jesus. He is still loved and still hated. Men still renounce their possessions and their lives, both for love of Him and out of hatred for Him. No living being today is quite so alive as He.

Probably the purpose of the life of Jesus and the extent of His influence can best be summarized by the apostate Renan who wrote: "Rest in Your glory, O noble Innovator. Your work is finished. Your divinity has been established. Fear no more that the edifice You have erected will fall through some error; from now on, immune from all frailty, You will watch from the peak of the divine peace the infinite consequences of Your acts. . . . For thousands of years the world will obey You; You will be the sign about which the fiercest battles of all will be waged. A thousand times more alive, a thousand times more beloved after Your death than during Your sojourn here below, You will become the cornerstone of Humanity, so much so that to tear Your name from the world would be to tumble it from its very foundation."

Let the world spend itself in giving verbal praise to Jesus; as for ourselves, we must carry on the work which He began. He left His Church in the hands of human beings because He had faith in us. Our hands must be His own in the world. On our feet He will continue to walk the earth. He has saved us. Now it is our life's work to save His Church and to love Him.